NEW 교원임용시험 전공영어 대비 [제1판]

Build Up

박문각 임용
동영상강의 www.pmg.co.kr

박현수 영어교육론 Ⅰ-2

Guideline for Pre-service Teachers
Classroom Teaching and Learning

Contents

Theoretical Background for Classroom Teaching

Chapter 05 교수법

Chapter 06 교재 개발 및 교재 분석

Chapter 07 Differentiated Instruction

Contents

I-2

Classroom Teaching and Learning

Build Up

Chapter
01

Receptive Skills

Chapter
01

Receptive Skills

01 \ Developing Skills and Strategies in Language Classroom

성공적인 언어 습득은 학습된 언어의 듣기, 읽기, 말하기, 쓰기가 효과적으로 이뤄지는 것이므로 교실 수업에서 교사는 듣기와 읽기의 receptive skills 및 말하기와 쓰기의 productive skills에 대한 원리와 실제 생활(real life)에서와 같은 언어 사용을 극대화해야 할 것이며, 학습 전략 및 사용 전략에 대한 탐구도 필요하다.

Traditionally we speak of four language skills: two 'receptive' skills—listening and reading, and two 'productive' skills—speaking and writing. The receptive skills have a number of things in common and the classroom techniques for reading and listening are often similar. In the same way, there are a number of similarities between lessons that practise the productive skills of speaking and writing.

Increasingly it is recognized that besides language skills students may also need to have learning skills—they may need to know how to learn. 'Learner development' (or 'learner training' as it is sometimes called) is concerned with helping students to become better, more independent learners.

1 Schema Theory

선험지식이론(schema theory)에 따르면 인간의 사전 경험과 사전 지식은 그와 관련된 새로운 경험과 지식을 이해하는 데 관여함으로써 새로운 지식을 받아들이는 데 영향을 끼친다.

Schema theory is based on the notion that past experiences lead to the creation of mental frameworks that help us make sense of new experiences. That is, prior knowledge and expectations that we bring to any situation are based on our background, education, and life experiences which shape our expectations and understanding of what we hear or read. There are two main types of schema. The first is *formal schema* and is based on the background

10   Chapter 01 Receptive Skills

knowledge of the structure of any given text. The second is *content schema* and relates to the background knowledge of the content area.

(1) Schemata

① **Content Schemata**: include general world knowledge, sociocultural knowledge, and topic knowledge

② **Formal Schemata**: consist of knowledge (rhetorical, discourse structure) we have of the overall structure of some speech event

> Ex : 'Once upon a time' heralds a certain kind of story which is likely to have a description of characters, and event, and outcome, and possibly a moral comment.

(2) Application of Skill Processing – Bottom-up and Top-down Processing

Reader나 listener가 text(or utterances)를 성공적으로 이해하기 위해서는 textual context상의 주요 어휘와 구문을 토대로 자신의 관련 경험과 지식을 활성화한 뒤 작가의 의도와 생각을 파악해 나가도록 필요에 따라 각각 bottom-up과 top-down 과정을 상호 보완적으로 사용해야 한다.

Processing a text can be seen as a two-way process between the text and the background knowledge or 'memory schemata' of the listener or reader. This again stresses the need to take the learner into account and suggests a more holistic approach to skills work. For example, the mind, when stimulated by key words or phrases in the text or by the context, activates a knowledge schema. That is, 'cognitive characteristics' of schema allow us to relate incoming information to existing information. Therefore, it makes sense that the more experience (both life and classroom) a learner has, the more available schemata they will have at their disposal and thus the better equipped they will be.

새로운 지식이나 정보를 이해하고 받아들이는 과정인 bottom-up과 top-down 과정은 상호 보완적으로 이루어져야 할 것이며, 한쪽으로 지나치게 치우칠 경우 전반적인 text comprehension에 도달하지 못할 것이다. 따라서, 교사는 학생들이 듣기나 읽기 과정에서 필요에 따라 두 가지 정보처리 능력(skills processing)을 가지고 보다 효과적인 text comprehension을 이룰 수 있도록 지도해야 한다.

In terms of receptive skills, there are two types of skill processing as follows: top-down and bottom-up processing. The former relates to making predictions based on background knowledge (knowledge-based) and the latter to 'building textual meaning from the individual linguistic units' (text-based). This has also been referred to as schematic knowledge, which is background knowledge that includes factual/sociological factors and procedural knowledge or how the language is used in discourse; versus systematic knowledge, which is the knowledge of the language system and includes semantic, syntactic and phonological features. All of which, when related by context, combine to provide comprehension.

Schema theory와 관련해 낯설고 익숙지 않은 form에 문제가 있을 때보다 content에 어려움이 있을 때 이해력이 현저히 떨어져 reading comprehension에 방해되는 것을 확인할 수 있다. 따라서, 교실에서 성공적인 recpetive skills을 키워 나가기 위해서 교사가 읽기나 듣기를 진행할 때 학습자가 구체적으로 이해할 수 있는 내용과 주제 선택이 우선적으로 이뤄져야 할 것이다.

So then, in relation to schema theory, it is with the former of both the above that we are most concerned. When only content or only form was unfamiliar, unfamiliar content caused more difficulty for the readers than did unfamiliar form. This has obvious implications for the classroom and language learning, and suggests the common sense idea that teachers should attempt to choose topics and texts which learners have some concrete understanding of, especially when it comes to actual content involved.

However, effective listening and reading skills involve both equally, working hand-in-hand in order to achieve the best results possible. For example, skilled readers (listeners) constantly adapt their mode of processing, changing to meet the demands of a particular text/reading (listening) situation; less skilled readers (listeners) tending to rely overly on processes in one direction and thus experiencing negative effects on overall comprehension. Overreliance on top-down processing has been referred to as 'schema interference', or a lack of understanding. When faced with unfamiliar topics, some students may 'overcompensate for absent schemata by reading in a slow, text-bound manner; other students may overcompensate by wild guessing'.

Meanwhile, most reading comprehension items only test bottom-up skills and fail to actually measure the way a reader (listeners) understands, advertising the use of 'recall protocols' in tests of reading comprehension. Therefore, we make sure that it is our responsibility as teachers to help make learners aware of the importance of both types in relation to one another and attempt to provide the right balance in order to achieve the greatest degree of comprehension possible.

(3) Application to Different Levels

선험지식을 활성화(activation of schematic knowledge)하기 위해 교사들은 듣기와 읽기 수업 과정 중에 학생들에게 pre-activities를 진행해야 한다. Pre-activities를 진행할 경우 학생들의 proficiency levels를 고려해 진행할 필요가 있는데, less competent students 에게는 language load를 줄이기 위한 pictorial activities(pictures)를 제공하고, more competent students에게는 가급적 non-pictorial activities를 진행하는 것이 보다 적절하다. 특히, beginner와 intermediate level 간에 이와 같은 고려가 더욱 필요하다. 또한, 가장 효과적인 schematic knowledge를 활성화시키는 방법은 여러 가지 pre-reading (listening) activities를 복합적으로 제공해 학생들로 하여금 기존의 배경지식과 새로운 배경지식을 모두 얻도록 하는 것이다.

Different pre-reading activities may be more or less effective with different proficiency levels. For low level students a more explicit pre-reading activity, such as discussing pictures and making predictions, can have a significantly greater facilitating effect on reading comprehension when compared to another less specific type; for example, vocabulary related.

Further, as lower level students may have the background knowledge but not the language skills to discuss them in English, their L1 might be used to access schemata but teachers should present the related vocabulary or otherwise a 'schema can be activated but learning the L2 can not be facilitated.' Teachers offer a variety of means in which relevant schemata may be constructed, including: discussion, real-life experiences, visual aids, text previewing, introduction and discussion of key vocabulary, and key-word/ concept association activities or brainstorming.

Although helpful, these pre-reading activities could be probably insufficient to be used only by themselves and teachers will almost certainly need to supply additional information; they can assume that pre-reading activities work best when used in a variety of combinations, believing that such activities must build both new background knowledge, as well as activating existing background knowledge.

2 Integrated Skills

In real life the language skills of listening, speaking, reading and writing are generally integrated rather than occurring in isolation. When taking part in a conversation, for example, we both listen and speak; when we fill in a form we read and write, and taking notes from a lecture involves listening and writing.

(1) Why is it useful to integrate skills?

통합 수업으로 진행되는 언어 학습은 학생들에게 실제와 근접한 언어 사용의 기회를 제공해 줄 수 있으며, 하나의 주제로 여러 언어 기능을 사용하게 해줌으로써 다양한 언어 활동을 할 수 있게 해준다. 또한, 주제에 대한 충분한 탐구와 해당 주제와 관련한 어휘가 반복적으로 사용되며 진정성 있는 연습(authentic practice)이 이뤄진다.

① An integrated skills lesson allows for the practice of language in a way which is closer to 'real world' and assists in the development of a full language user.

② A lesson which integrated a number of skills has more variety.

③ It gives an opportunity for a topic to be fully explored and for vocabulary connected to the topic to be practised and recycled.

(2) Classroom Examples

① **Intermediate level**: A lesson for intermediate level students based around a newspaper article might include the following stages: speaking → reading → writing

ⓐ **Step 1**: The teacher introduces the topic (perhaps by showing pictures) and elicits what the students know and/or think about the subject.

ⓑ **Step 2**: The students could discuss what they would expect to find in an article on the topic in question.

ⓒ **Step 3**: The students read the newspaper article. Tasks could focus on assisting comprehension and perhaps a more detailed study of some of the vocabulary, or on the style of the article.

ⓓ **Step 4**: The students could write a letter to the editor in response to the article, or write an article on the same subject from a different perspective, or in a different style.

② **Lower level**: A lesson for <u>lower level</u> students about finding accommodation might include following stages: reading → speaking → listening → writing

    ⓐ **Step 1**: Low level students start with the reading of a newspaper advertisement (with a focus on some of the special vocabulary).

    ⓑ **Step 2**: Low level students go on to a roleplay/information gap activity in which the prospective tenant telephones the landlord/lady to ask questions and to make an appointment to see the flat.

    ⓒ **Step 3**: Low level students listen to a text of someone being shown round the flat.

    ⓓ **Step 4**: Low level students write a letter to a friend describing their new flat.

Plus ➕

Models of Skills Integration

1. Content-based Instruction

It integrates the learning of some specific subject matter content with the learning of a second language. Content-based teaching allows learners to acquire knowledge and skills that transcend all the bits and pieces of language that may occupy hours and days of analyzing in a traditional language classroom.

2. Theme-based Instruction

Theme-based instruction is not the same as content-based. The differences of them are the primary content-based's purpose of a course is to instruct students in a subject-matter area, and language is of secondary, and subordinate interest. Theme-based instruction offers an alternative to traditional language classes by organizing the course around themes or topics, equally emphasizing both content and language objectives.

Here are some possible theme-based activities:

① Use environmental statistics and facts for classroom reading, writing, discussion, and debate.

② Carry out research and writing projects.

③ Have students create their own environmental awareness material.

④ Arrange field trips.

⑤ Conduct simulation games.

3. Experiential Learning

Emphasis on two principles:

① One learns best by doing, by active experimentation.

② Inductive learning by discovery activates strategies that enable students to take charge of their own learning processes.

Experiential learning implies a direct encounter with the subject matter or topic being studied. Experiential learning techniques tend to be learner-centered by nature. Experiential learning tends to put an emphasis on the psychomotor aspects of language learning by involving learners in physical actions in which language is subsumed and reinforced.

4. The Episode Hypothesis

The episode hypothesis contributes or relates to integrated-skills teaching. Here are some possible ways:

① Stories or episodes challenge the teacher and textbook writer to present interesting, natural language.

② Episodes can be presented in either written or spoken form.

③ Episodes can provide the stimulus for spoken or written questions that students respond to, in turn, by speaking or writing.

④ Students can be encouraged to write their own episodes, or to complete an episode whose resolution or climax is not presented.

⑤ Those written episodes might then be dramatized in the classroom by the students.

5. Task-based Language Teaching(TBLT)

In task-based instruction, the priority is not the forms of language, but rather the functional purposes for which language must be used. Course goals in TBLT are not linguistic in the traditional sense of just focusing on grammar or phonology; The course goals center on learners' pragmatic language competence, by maintaining the centrality of functions like exchanging opinions, reading newspapers and menus, writing letters and e-mails, etc.

3) Classroom Organization

(1) Whole Class

일제식 수업(whole class work)은 학생들에게 소속감을 제공하고 low level 학생들에 대한 통제적 연습 활동에는 매우 유용하다. 하지만 전체 학생들 앞에서 자신의 performance를 보여줘야 한다는 학습 부담감이 있으며, 각 학생들에게 부여되는 참여의 기회가 적고, 특히 토의 등의 학습에는 부적절한 교실 구성이다.

This is useful for presenting information and for controlled practice (such as repetition and drilling) which is often used, especially at lower levels. Whole class teaching can be dynamic and motivating and by treating everyone as part of the same group, we can build a great sense of belonging—of being part of a team.

However, when a class is working as a whole group, it is necessarily the case that individual students get fewer individual opportunities either to speak or to reflect. Whole-class teaching is less effective if we want to encourage individual contributions and discussion, since speaking out in front of a whole class is often more demanding—and therefore more inhibiting—than speaking in smaller groups.

(2) Group Work and Pair Work

일제식 수업(whole class work)의 경우 학습에 대한 학생들의 적극적인 참여와 주도적인 역할을 기대할 수 없으므로, 현 교실 수업에서는 소집단(small groups) 형태로 교실을 구성해 각 그룹별로 제공된 과제를 토대로 소집단 구성원의 각 역할을 충실히 수행하도록 하고 있다.

Group work and pair work both foster <u>cooperative activity</u> in the students involved work together to complete a task. They may be discussing a topic, doing a role-play or working at a computer in order to find information from a website for a webquest or they may be writing up a report.

In pairs and groups, students tend to participate more actively, and they also have more chance to experiment with the language than is possible in a whole-class arrangement. Both pair work and group work give the students chances for greater independence. Because the students are working together without the teacher controlling every move, they take some of their own learning decisions, they decide what language to use to complete a certain task and they can work without the pressure of the whole class listening to what they are doing.

① 장점

ⓐ Group work generates interactive language.

일제식 수업은 학생들에게 충분한 언어 사용 기회를 주지 못하지만 소집단 활동은 학생들이 자유롭게 자신의 생각을 주고받을 수 있으므로 실제 언어 사용 기회를 극대화시켜 상호작용적인 언어를 생성한다.

ⓑ Group work offers an embracing affective climate.

일제식 수업은 학생들을 호명했을 때 학생들이 준비 없이 발화의 기회를 얻게 되기도 하고, 공개적인 발표(public display)에 학생들의 정의적 여과막(affective filter)이 높아질 수 있으나, 소집단 활동은 학생들의 preference, proficiency level, interest 등의 개인차(individual difference)를 반영해 소집단을 조직함으로써 학생들의 정의적 분위기에서 학습 활동을 극대화할 수 있다.

ⓒ Group work promotes learner responsibility and autonomy.

소집단을 the same ability grouping으로 구성할 경우, 각 그룹에 맞는 level-appropriate task를 제공함으로써 학생들이 어려움 없이 과업에 적극적으로 임하게 된다. 또한, 소집단을 mixed level grouping으로 구성할 경우, 서로 수준이 다른 학생들에게 각각 수준별 역할을 제공해 group 내 자신의 역할을 주도적으로 이끌어 나가며 각자 학습에 대한 책임감과 자율성을 키워줄 수 있다.

ⓓ Group work is a step toward individualizing instruction.

소집단 활동은 현 교실의 가장 어려운 과제 중 하나인 수준별 수업(level-differentiated class)을 위한 대안책 중 하나이다. 즉, 학생들을 동일한 level끼리 묶어(same-ability grouping) 각 수준에 맞는 수업을 함으로써 개별화 학습으로 나가는 첫 단계가 될 수 있다.

② 단점

ⓐ The teacher is no longer in control of the class.

대집단 수업만을 진행한 교사일 경우 소집단으로 수업을 진행할 때 각 그룹별로 진행되는 과정이나 문제점들에 대해 적절히 대처하기 어려울 수 있다. 따라서 이 경우에는 각 group leader를 뽑아 그룹 내에서 생길 수 있는 문제를 대처할 수 있도록 수업을 운영한다.

ⓑ Students will use their native language.

아직 중간언어의 영어 체계를 가지고 있는 학생들은 소집단 활동에서 자신의 생각 등을 표현할 때 (적절하게 영어로 표현하기 어려울 경우) 모국어를 빈번하게 사용할 수 있다. 이 경우, 교사는 의사소통 장애가 생길 때 해결할 수 있는 여러 가지 communication strategies에 대한 지도와 훈련을 통해 학생들의 모국어 사용을 줄여 나갈 수 있다.

ⓒ Students' errors will be reinforced in small groups.

부정확한 언어체계를 가진 상태에서의 언어 사용에는 당연히 오류가 출현할 수밖에 없다. 따라서 교사는 학생들의 과업이 모두 끝난 후, 반복적이고 많은 학생들이 공통적으로 범하는 오류에 대한 follow-up treatment에서 corrective feedback을 제공하도록 한다.

ⓓ Teachers cannot monitor all groups at once.

학생들이 소집단에서 과업을 진행할 때 교사는 교실을 돌아다니며 학생들의 과업에 대한 참여도나 어려움 등을 monitoring하게 된다. 하지만, 동시에 모든 그룹에 대한 monitoring과 language support를 제공할 수 없다는 사실을 인지해야 한다. 따라서 각 group에 monitor를 담당하는 group role를 부여하는 것이 필요하다.

ⓔ Some learners prefer to work alone.

일부 학생들은 소집단 활동보다 개인 학습 활동을 더 선호할 수 있다. 따라서 교사는 융통성 있는 과업 운영을 하도록 한다. 가령, 소집단 활동과 개별 활동을 병행해 진행하는 수업 운영 방식을 취할 수 있다.

ⓕ Diverse student learning styles complicate group work.

학생들의 preference, interest 등의 개별적 차이가 소집단 활동을 복잡하고 어렵게 만들 수 있다.

Plus ⊕

1. Personalizing Learning with Flexible Grouping

Flexible instructional grouping is specifically intended to provide a better instructional match between students and their individual needs. It is a critical management strategy in a differentiated classroom. It lets a teacher personalize learning activities according to students' needs, and, in the process, gives her time to provide additional instruction or extended learning experiences to particular students or groups. In fact, students feel more involved, engaged, and confident when they're involved in activities tailored to their learning needs and preferences.

2. Flexible Grouping Compared with Other Grouping Strategies

Flexible grouping is just one of several techniques for responding to learner differences.

① **Ability grouping**: Students are grouped according to scores on placement tests. That is, students are grouped according to general learning abilities, rather than particular talents or limitation, for example, in math or language arts.

② **Cooperative grouping**: Students are grouped for collaborative work, either by the teacher or by student choice.

③ **Flexible instructional grouping**: Students are grouped according to their learning needs, strengths, and preferences. Grouping is changed regularly to match student needs to the task at hand.

④ **Performance grouping**: Students are grouped according to grades or performance in a particular subject area—for example, accelerated, enriched, or advanced placement classes.

4 Teacher's Role

(1) The Controller

The teacher is in complete charge of the class, what students do, what they say and how they say it. The teacher assumes this role when a new language is being introduced and accurate reproduction and drilling techniques are needed.

01

In this classroom, the teacher is mostly the center of focus, the teacher may have the gift of instruction, and can inspire through their own knowledge and expertise, but, does this role really allow for enough student talk time? Is it really enjoyable for the learners? There is also a perception that this role could have a lack of variety in its activities.

(2) The Prompter (Facilitator)

The teacher encourages students to participate and makes suggestions about how students may proceed in an activity. The teacher should be helping students only when necessary.

When learners are literally 'lost for words', the prompter can encourage by discreetly nudging students. Students can sometimes lose the thread or become unsure how to proceed; the prompter in this regard can prompt but always in a supportive way.

(3) The Resource

The teacher is a kind of walking resource center ready to offer help if needed, or provide learners with whatever language they lack when performing communicative activities. The teacher must make her/himself available so that learners can consult her/him when (and only when) it is absolutely necessary.

As a resource the teacher can guide learners to use available resources such as the internet, for themselves, it certainly isn't necessary to spoon-feed learners, as this might have the downside of making learners reliant on the teacher.

(4) The Assessor

The teacher assumes this role to see how well students are performing or how well they performed. Feedback and correction are organized and carried out.

There are a variety of ways we can grade learners, the role of an assessor gives teachers an opportunity to correct learners. However, if it is not communicated with sensitivity and support it could prove counter-productive to a student's self-esteem and confidence in learning the target language.

(5) The Organizer

This is perhaps the most difficult and important role the teacher has to play. The success of many activities depends on good organization and on the students knowing exactly what they are to do next. Giving instructions is vital in this role as well as setting up activities.

The organizer can also serve as a demonstrator, this role also allows a teacher to get involved and engaged with learners. The teacher also serves to open and neatly close activities and also give content feedback.

(6) The Participant

This role improves the atmosphere in the class when the teacher takes part in an activity. However, the teacher takes a risk of dominating the activity when performing it.

Here the teacher can enliven a class; if a teacher is able to stand back and not become the center of attention, it can be a great way to interact with learners without being too overpowering.

(7) The Tutor

The teacher acts as a coach when students are involved in project work or self-study. The teacher provides advice and guidance and helps students clarify ideas and limit tasks.

This role can be a great way to pay individual attention to a student. It can also allow a teacher to tailor—make a course to fit specific student needs. However, it can also lead to a student becoming too dependent or even too comfortable with one teacher and one method or style of teaching.

02 \ Teaching Listening

과거 listening은 소극적인 과정으로 이해됐으나, 최근 경향은 listening을 적극적이고 상호작용적인 과정으로 바라보고 있으며 교실에서 listening 수업도 적극적인 듣기 역할에 초점을 두고 있다.

Listening was traditionally seen as a passive process by which the listener receives information sent by a speaker. More recent models view listening as a much more active and interpretive process in which the message is not fixed but is created in the interactional space between participants. Meanings are shaped by context and constructed by the listener through the act of interpreting meaning rather than receiving it intact.

1 Types of Listening

(1) One-way Listening (Transactional Talk)

전달하는 내용에 집중을 요하는 <u>사실적 정보와 명제 등을 전달하기 위한 대화</u>로, 실생활에서 언어 행위의 결과를 유도한다.

Transactional dialogue, carried out for the purpose of conveying or <u>exchanging specific information</u>, is an extended form of responsive language.

> Ex T: What is the main idea in this essay?
>   S: The United Nations should have more authority.
>   T: More authority than what?
>   S: Than it does right now....

① business-type talk

② message-oriented

③ the focus on content and conveying factual or propositional information

> Ex giving instructions, explaining, describing, giving directions, ordering, inquiring, requesting, relating, checking on the correctness of details, verifying understanding

(2) **Two-way Listening** (Interactional Talk)

상호작용을 촉진시키기 위한 대화로, message 그 자체보다 화자와 화자들 간의 관계에 그 목적이 있다.

Interpersonal dialogue is carried out more for the purpose of <u>maintaining social relationships</u> than for the transmission of facts and information.

> **Ex** Amy : Hi, Bob, how's it going?
> Bob : Oh, so-so.
> Amy : Not a great weekend, huh?
> Bob : Well, far be it from me to criticize, but I'm pretty miffed about last week….

① social type talk
② person-oriented
③ the establishment and maintenance of cordial social relationship

> **Ex** making small talk with a coworker or talking to a friend about a concern at home

(3) Implications for Instruction

① Teachers need to provide practice experiences in both transactional talk and interactional talk.
② Students need instruction and listening practice to help them recognize when one of the two functions is operating and how they can respond appropriately.

2 Listening – Problems and Solutions

다수의 학습자들은 동일한 내용을 읽는 것보다 듣는 경우 더 어려움을 느낀다. 이는 듣기는 눈 깜짝할 사이에 지나가지만 읽기는 원하는 시간 동안 반복해서 읽을 수 있기 때문이다.

(1) Linguistic Features

① **Liaison**: the linking of words in speech when the second word begins with a vowel

> Ex *an orange* /@nOrIndZ/

② **Elision**: leaving out a sound or sounds

> Ex *suppose* may be pronounced /sp@uz/ in rapid speech

These are common phenomena that make it difficult for students to distinguish or recognize individual words in the stream of speech. They are used to seeing words written as discrete entities in their textbooks.

③ **Colloquial words and expressions**: Most students who have been exposed mainly to formal or bookish English may not be familiar with these expressions.

> Ex *stuff* for material, *guy* for man

④ **Redundant utterances**: In spontaneous conversation people sometimes uses ungrammatical sentences because of nervousness or hesitation. They may omit elements of sentences or add something redundant. This may make it difficult for the listener to understand the meaning. Redundant utterances may take the form of repetitions, false starts, re-phrasings, self-corrections, elaborations and apparently meaningless additions such as *I mean* or *you know*. This redundancy is a natural feature of speech and may be either a help or a hindrance, depending on the students' level.

(2) Listener

Foreign-language students are not familiar enough with cliches and collocations in English to predict a missing word or phrase. They cannot, for example, be expected to know that *rosy* often collocates with *cheeks* nor to predict the last word will be something like *rage* when they hear the phrase *he was in a towering...* This is a major problem for students.

Lack of sociocultural, factual and contextual knowledge of the target language can present an obstacle to comprehension because language is used to express its culture.

Plus ➕

Solutions

1. Grade listening materials according to the students' level and provide authentic materials rather than idealized, filtered samples. It is true that natural speech is hard to grade and it is difficult for students to follow whole meaning.

   Nevertheless, the materials should progress step by step from semi-authenticity that displays most of the linguistic features of natural speech to total authenticity, because the final aim is to understand natural speech in real life.

2. Design task-oriented exercises to engage the students' interest and help them learn listening skills and strategies subconsciously.

3 Effective Listening Lesson

(1) Pre-listening Stage(듣기 전 단계)

선험지식을 활성화하고 하향식 과정(top-down)을 자극한다.

This stage is to prepare the learners for what they are going to hear, just as we are usually prepared in real life (for example, we usually have expectations about the topic, and even the language). Thus, before a listening activity, encourage the students to think about and discuss what they are going to hear. Use prompts such as realia, visuals, questions, references to the students' experiences, a short discussion tasks to arouse the students' interest, to activate any knowledge they have about the topic and to help them predict what they are going to hear.

Example

Job Interview Clinic

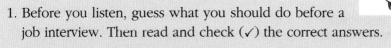

Job counselor: Greetings. Today I want to give you some tips on how to make a good impression at a job interview with an international company.

1. Before you listen, guess what you should do before a job interview. Then read and check (✓) the correct answers.

   Job Interview: Before the interview...
   ☐ a. Don't prepare too much for the interview.
   ☐ b. Think about all the reasons why you want the job.
   ☐ c. Prepare for questions about work experience, strong and weak points, and special skills.
   ☐ d. Don't try to think of other questions the interviewer might ask.
   ☐ e. Don't think of a question to ask the interviewer because this is not polite.

Plus ➕

Before Listening

1. Think about the topic of the text. (brainstorming)
2. Read/focus on the title.
3. Consider your own knowledge.
4. Think about the type of text.
5. Predict what your expect to hear about.

(2) **While-listening Stage(듣기 중 전략)**

While they listen, students will need to be involved in an <u>authentic purpose</u> for listening and encouraged to attend to the text more intensively or more extensively, <u>for gist or for specific information</u>. For example, a wide repertoire of activity types is possible: taking multiple-choice items, filling a chart, matching pictures with the text, or drawing a picture or making notes. For learners in early stages of developing listening ability, simple activities such as ticking a list or numbering pictures in the correct order will prevent the anxiety and demotivation arising from trying to write while listening.

① Comprehension process

ⓐ Bottom-up processing proceeds from sounds to words, to grammatical relationships to lexical meanings, etc., to a final "message."

ⓑ Top-down processing is evoked from "a bank of prior knowledge and global expectations and other background information (schemata) that the listener brings to the text.

 **In the Classroom**

Sample Lesson: Top-down and Bottom-up in the Classroom

실제 교실 상황에서는 효과적인 듣기 전략 지도를 위해 두 가지 전략을 모두 사용한다. 전형적인 듣기 수업은 하향식 전략에서 시작해 상향식으로 다가가는데, 다음과 같이 전개될 수 있다.

Procedure	Why?
Discuss the general topic	Learners start to think about the topic, raising a number of issues that will be discussed later on the recording. This preparation may help them to hear these things being discussed later.
Predict the specific content	Students hypothesize specific issues that may be raised.
Predict the structure	Students consider/discuss possible organizational structures for a phone-in (who speaks? what kind of questions? typical exchanges? etc). This may help learners to recognize the content more easily.
Gist listening for overview	Learners get an overall impression of the content without worrying about small items or individual words.
Gist listening for attitudes	Learners interpret intonation, paralinguistic features.
More careful listening for complex meanings	By catching and interpreting smaller parts of the text, learners fine-tune their understanding.
Listening to pick out specific small language details	This focused work (e.g. on pronunciation) may raise learner awareness (e.g. of weak forms) and thus help students to listen better in future.

② Listening strategies

ⓐ **Listening for global understanding or gist**: to give learners practice in understanding only the main ideas of a passage. It is not always necessary for us to understand the details of what we listen to.

> Ex   a. Is the speaker describing a vacation or a day in the office?
>   b. Is the radio report about news or weather?
>   c. Why is the speaker asking the main questions?
>   d. Did the speaker like or dislike the movie?

ⓑ **Listening for specific information (scanning)**: to let listeners pick out specific information in a text without expecting them to understand every word

Listening for specific information is one of the most common tasks in the listening classroom. Listening for specifics isn't limited to literal processing, but often they go together. While literal understanding is the lowest level of processing, it doesn't mean it is unimportant. Much of the information we get day-to-day we get through literal processing.

ⓒ **Listening for detail**: to practice listening intensively for details of the text

The types of activities are similar to the ones of listening for gist and specific information. Difference is the content of the questions. Listening for specific information with news headlines might entail simply identifying the countries mentioned and the event that occurred in each one. A more detailed listening could require learners to identify the players, the time, or the exact location of the events.

ⓓ **Making inference**: analyzing, interpreting and evaluating the meaning of a text

Inferencing is a higher level listening skill. However, it is a mistake to wait until learners are at an intermediate level or above to begin working on it. Indeed, beginning learners lack the large vocabulary and grammatical knowledge that they will have later, so they need to "listen between lines" at their level.

(3) Post-listening Stage(듣기 후 단계)

들은 내용을 바르게 이해했는지 확인하거나 들은 내용을 말하기나 읽기 등 다른 기능으로 통합해 듣기 수업을 마무리한다.

Post-listening activities can take students into a more intensive phase of study in which aspects of bottom-up listening are practised. It can involve integration with other skills through developing the topic into reading, speaking, or writing activities. The whole class checks answers to pre-set questions and responds to the content of the passage.

4 Listening Activities

(1) Jigsaw Listening

In three groups, students listen to three different tapes, all of which are about the same thing (*witness reports after an accident or a crime, phone conversations arranging a meeting, different news stories which explain a strange events, etc.*). Students have to assemble all the facts by comparing notes. In this way, they may find out what actually happened, solve a mystery or get a rounded account of a situation or topic.

(2) Dictogloss

들은 내용을 바탕으로 이야기를 재구성하도록 하는 dictogloss 활동은 상향식 듣기 과정과 하향식 듣기 과정을 모두 필요로 하는 대표적인 통합형 과제(integrative task)이다.

① The dictogloss technique provides a useful bridge between bottom-up and top-down listening.

② The dictogloss aims to provide an opportunity for learners to use their productive grammar in the task of text creation. Also, it aims to encourage learners to find out what they do and do not know English. This is realized in the attempts to reconstruct the text and in the subsequent analysis of those attempts.

③ Learners who regularly engage in dictogloss will gradually see a refinement in their global aural comprehension and note-taking skills.

• Required Steps for a Dictogloss Activity •

Step	Students	Teacher
1. Preparation	• Study vocabulary activities to prepare for the text. • Discuss the topic (predict vocabulary and content etc.). • Move into groups.	
2. Listening for meaning	Listen to the whole text.	Reads the text at normal speed.
3. Listening and note-taking	Take notes listing key words.	Reads again at normal speed.
4. Text reconstruction in group	Work in groups to reconstruct an approximation of the text from notes (one learner acts as the writer).	• Helps groups. • Offers guidelines.
5. Text comparison between groups	Compare group version of the text. Pay attention to points of usage that emerge from the discussion.	• Facilitates class comparison of versions from different groups. • Facilitates discussion and correction of errors.

* Steps 4 and 5 encourage learners to pay close attention to language form (i.e, word forms, word order, spelling, grammar rules, etc.)

Plus ➕

Form-focused Instruction of Task-based Instruction

과제 기반 수업은 학습자에게 의미와 유창성을 길러 나가도록 하는 수업 모형이나, 과업 후 진행되는 언어 형태에 대한 정확성을 길러 나가도록 한다는 측면에서 의사소통 교수의 주요 원리인 fluency와 accuracy를 함께 키워 줄 수 있는 수업 모형이다. 특히, focus on form approach 측면에서 과제 기반 언어 형태에 대한 초점을 맞추는 방식으로 collaborative task인 dictogloss가 권장되고 있다.

(3) Information Transfer

듣기 활동으로 입력된 특정 정보의 형태를 달리 표현하는 활동으로, 듣고 난 뒤 그리기 (listen and draw)와 테이블 채우기(filling in the table)가 대표적이다.

Learners reproduce the message they hear in a new form, for example, when they listen and respond by ordering a set of pictures, completing a map, drawing a picture or completing a table.

① Most information transfer activities focus the learners' attention on the details of the information used in the activity.

② It encourages meaning-focused listening and supports listening.

③ It focuses learners' attention on listening without the extra burden of having to read a list of questions or write long answers.

Example

Listen and fill in the blanks with the correct information about Minsu's schedule.

Things to do	Monday	Tuesday	Wednesday	Thursday	Friday
Morning					
Afternoon					

⑤ Extensive vs. Intensive Listening

A distinction can be drawn between *intensive* and *extensive listening*. As with reading, *extensive listening* refers to listening which the students often do away from the classroom, *for pleasure* or some other reason. The audio materials they consume in this way—often on CDs, on MP3 players, DVDs, videos or on the Internet—should consist of texts that they can enjoy listening to because they more or less understand them without the intervention of a teacher or course materials to help them. *Intensive listening* is different from extensive listening in that students listen specifically in order to work on listening skills, and in order to study the way in which English is spoken. It usually takes place in classrooms or language laboratories, and typically occurs when teachers are present to guide students through any listening difficulties, and point them to areas of interest.

(1) Extensive Listening

담화 내용의 전체적인 의미를 이해하는 것을 목적으로 하는 듣기를 말한다. 주로 학습자들이 자신이 들을 자료를 선택하며 **교실 수업 상황 밖**에서 이뤄진다.

① Teachers encourage students to choose for themselves what they listen to and to do the listening for pleasure and general language improvement.

② Extensive listening usually takes place outside the classroom.

③ Students listen to a lot of easy materials with a minimal task or no task at all.

④ Materials for extensive listening can be obtained from a number of sources: smartphone apps, CD, broadcasts online, etc.

⑤ It is useful for increasing motivation, listening, pronunciation, and good speaking habits.

(2) Intensive Listening

담화 내용을 바탕으로 특정한 정보를 찾거나 언어 자질에 대한 학습을 목적으로 하는 **수 업 상황**에서 이뤄지는 듣기 활동을 말한다.

① It allows students the opportunity to focus on discrete points of the language and to develop listening skills.

② Intensive listening usually takes place in the classroom with teachers' preparation.

③ It can include replaying a recording several times, which encourages students to get as much information as is necessary or appropriate from a single hearing.

④ Comprehension questions which focus on detailed information.
   ⓐ **Literal comprehension**: where the answer is clearly stated somewhere in the passage.
   ⓑ **Inferential comprehension**: where the student has to make some sort of connection for himself. This can facilitate connection between something in the passage and the students' knowledge of the outside world.
   ⓒ **Critical (personal) comprehension**: where the question is related to the student's own experience or opinion.

6 Classroom Implications

How can teachers help the students to understand a listening text?

(1) Choose a text which will interest the students and formulate aims that are suitable for their level and needs. Examples of specific aims are:

① To develop global listening skills
② To develop intensive listening skills
③ To set the context for a roleplay
④ To introduce a vocabulary 'set' in a natural context

(2) Focus on general or global understanding before detailed understanding. It is essential to build up knowledge of the text gradually—to start with what the students already know in order to tackle the new, to begin with the easy aspects and go on to the more difficult.

(3) Encourage the students to use what they already know (their knowledge of the world and of English) to help them infer meaning. Before they listen, help them to predict what they are going to hear by activating any knowledge they may have of the topic or situation. Elicit the sort of language they expect to be used. It may be helpful to revise or teach some key items of vocabulary that appear in the listening if they are important to an understanding of the text.

① Guess how the speakers are feeling by their intonation.
② Get information about the structure of the text from the intonation.
③ Guess the situation from any background noises.
④ Use any visual clues available.
⑤ Listen out for familiar words which give a clue to the topic or situation.
⑥ Guess any unknown words from the context.

(4) Give plenty of support, especially with lower level students or those who are not confident about listening. For example, some teachers like to let students read the tapescript for an authentic text if it is available usually after they have listened to it or while they are listening to it a second time. Occasionally a weak class or one at the beginning of the course can read a tapescript, or part of it, in advance. They can do activities such as sorting out the jumbled lines in tapescripts, or filling in gaps in tapescripts, to help them prepare for what they are going to hear.

(5) Motivate the students by choosing texts that are interesting and that provide a real incentive for the students to understand and to contribute their own ideas and opinions.

(6) Choose tasks for the students to do before and while listening rather than afterwards. In that way teachers are focusing on understanding rather than just good memory.

03 \ Teaching Reading

1970년 이후 의사소통 능력의 배양을 주 목적으로 한 의사소통 중심의 교수법과 인지주의 심리학의 영향으로 인해 <u>학습자 중심의 교육으로 선회함에 따라 학습의 결과보다는 학습의 과정이 더 중시됐다.</u> 이러한 경향으로 읽기 지도도 과거의 *text-based*에서 *reader-based*로 바뀌며 독자가 그 내용을 어떻게 이해하고 평가하는지에 더 많은 관심을 갖게 됐다. 이러한 관점에서 읽기는 단순히 사실을 이해하는 능력뿐만 아니라 텍스트 내에 주어진 정보를 분석하고 종합할 수 있는 능력을 필요로 하는 복합적이고 다각적인 사고 과정으로 받아들여지게 됐다.

As the receptive skills, one of the key similarities between reading and listening is the important role *prior knowledge* plays in order to understand and use written or oral texts, which is called *schema theory*.

> ▶ **Prior knowledge** and expectations that we bring to any situation are based on our cultural background, education, and life experiences. We have 'scripts' in our mind about how events in the world unfold, and these scripts are called "*schemata*." Schema theory suggests that prior knowledge shapes our expectation and understanding of what we hear or read. The closer our schema is to the content of what we hear or read, the easier it will be for us to understand.

Therefore, in a language classroom, teachers need to provide "advance organizer"—pedagogical devices that activate relevant background knowledge—to facilitate the learning and retention of new material at the stage of pre-listening or pre-reading.

• Figure 1. A One-way View of Reading •

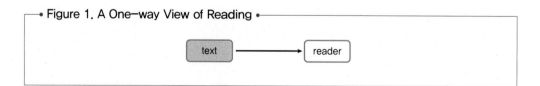

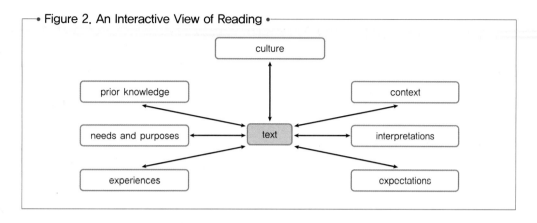

• Figure 2. An Interactive View of Reading •

As with listening, an efficient reader is one who can draw the information they need from the whole text using top-down processing.

> ▶ **Top-down processing** is where a global meaning of the text is obtained, through "clues" in the text and the reader's good schematic knowledge. This is related to the skills reading not word for word but whole meaning quickly and efficiently.

On the other hand, slow or poor readers rely heavily on decoding letters, words, and sentences which is called bottom-up processing. That is, they build up meaning by reading word for word, letter for letter, carefully scrutinizing both vocabulary and syntax.

읽기 과정이란 텍스트의 단어들을 정확하고 빠르게 인식하는 상향식(bottom-up)과 독자의 예측 및 추측의 과정을 중심으로 의미를 파악하는 하향식(top-down)이 상호작용해 계속적으로 일어나는 과정이다. 그러나 학생들이 지나치게 상향식에 치우칠 경우 글의 전체적인 맥락이나 작가의 의도 및 함축적인 의미를 파악하고 어휘의 사회 문화적 의미를 이해하기 어렵다. 반면, 지나치게 하향식에 치우칠 경우 자신의 선험지식과 지나친 추측으로 인해 정확한 읽기가 진행되기 어렵다. 따라서 교사는 읽기 지도 시 학생들에게 필요에 따라 두 가지 이해 과정(top-down+bottom-up)을 적절하게 상호 보완적으로 사용하도록 지도해야 할 것이다.

Reading, like listening and speaking, is interactive in nature and open to various interpretations. A text does not just transmit information, as shown in Figure 2. It involves information going from the text to the reader and back. During the reading readers, first, can adopt top-down processing to predict the probable meaning, then moving to the bottom-up processing to check whether that is really what the writer says. Also, the bottom-up processing can sometimes occur when the readers' schematic knowledge is inadequate.

1 Simplified vs. Authentic Texts

The pedagogical benefits of using authentic vs. simplified readings have long been an issue of debate and concern so far.

> • What kind of text do you prefer to use in your classroom and why?
> • Which kind do your students enjoy more?
> • Which type of reading can help us promote reading beyond the classroom?

교실에서 학생들의 성공적인 언어 학습을 위해 simplified texts를 사용해야 하는지 또는 authentic texts를 사용해야 하는지에 대한 논의는 중요한 교육학적 문제로 끊임없이 대두돼 왔다. 현재 진행되는 교실 수업에서의 언어 학습 목적이 실질적인 의사소통 증진이라는 측면에서 본다면 교실의 teaching materials 선정 기준은 당연히 진정성 (authenticity)이 될 것이다.

"It has been traditionally supposed that the language presented to learners should be simplified in some way for easy access and acquisition. Nowadays there are recommendations that the language presented should be authentic." (Widdowson)

Authentic texts have been generally defined as texts "originally created by a real speaker or writer for a real audience and designed to convey a real message", whereas simplified texts generally refer to texts created "to illustrate a specific language feature … to modify the amount of new lexical input introduced to learners; or to control for propositional input, or a combination thereof."

> ▶ **Authentic texts** are those which are designed not for language students, but for the speakers of the language in question.

Communicative language teaching prominently features the use of authentic materials with the pedagogical goal that learners will be exposed to real language used in real contexts (Larsen-Freeman, 2002). The influence and strong trend toward communicative language teaching over the past four decades has led teaching professionals to prefer the use of authentic texts, despite the lack of empirical evidence to support their superiority over simplified texts. Other theories or approaches that have been cited in favour of the use of authentic materials include, for example, Krashen's input hypothesis, which suggests that "natural communicative input is the key to designing a syllabus" (n.d., para 11).

The whole language instructional approach also focuses on using authentic materials in the process of facilitating language development (Richards & Rodgers, 2001, p. 113) and on the need for language learners to be introduced to enriched context and to experience language in its totality (Goodman, 1986).

The major perceived benefit of using authentic texts lies in the way it makes it possible to introduce natural and contextualized language to learners (Larsen-Freeman, 2002). At the same time, many arguments against the use of authentic texts centre on their linguistic difficulty, such as lexical and syntactic complexity and conceptual and cultural density. A quite few proponents prefer the use of simplified texts to authentic ones with major theoretical support from, for example, Krashen's comprehensible input and affective filter hypotheses.

The former states that "the learner improves and progresses along the 'natural order' when he/she receives second language 'input' that is one step beyond his/her current stage of linguistic competence, which simplified texts arguably are able to provide" for beginning and intermediate learners. The latter theory asserts that a high level of motivation and low level of anxiety facilitate better second-language acquisition. As such, appropriately selected simplified texts presumably could motivate learners more than authentic texts, which might be overly challenging for learners with lower proficiency levels. In addition to making texts more comprehensible, simplified texts are thought to facilitate learning by excluding distracting idiosyncratic styles and offering enhanced redundancy and elaborated explanation.

In conclusion, however, most educators agree that <u>using authentic materials</u> is unquestionably a better practice in second-language reading instruction.

따라서, 교사는 교실 수업에서 진정성 있는 학습 자료(authentic materials)를 선택할 경우 다음과 같은 요인을 고려해야 한다. 가령, 이해할 수 없을 정도의 언어적 어려움 없이 학습자의 학습을 독려할 수 있는지, 자연스러운 맥락 안에 구어 또는 문어의 적절한 용례가 제시됐는지, 특정한 요소 학습을 포함시키기 위해 과도하게 자료가 왜곡됐는지 등을 살펴봐야 할 것이다.

(1) Important Factors in Choosing Authentic Reading Materials

① **Suitability of Content**: 학생들의 흥미를 끌면서 학습의 목적에 적합한 내용을 담고 있어야 한다.

Materials that students will find interesting, enjoyable, challenging, and appropriate for their goals in learning English.

ⓐ Does the text interest the students?

ⓑ Is it relevant to the students' need?

ⓒ Does it represent the type of material that the student will use outside of the classroom?

② **Exploitability**: 학생들의 과업과 언어 기능을 개발시키는 데 도움이 돼야 하며 다른 기능과 통합 가능해야 한다.

A text that facilitates the achievement of certain language and content goals, that is exploitable for instructional tasks and techniques, and that is integratable with other skills.

ⓐ Can the text be exploited for teaching purpose?

ⓑ For what purpose should the text be exploited?

ⓒ What skills/strategies can be developed by exploiting the text?

③ **Readability**: 텍스트의 단어와 문장의 구조가 학생들에게 지나치게 어렵거나 쉽지 않은 수준이어야 한다.

A text with lexical and structural difficulty that will challenge students without overwhelming them. Since the language of a text may be difficult for one student and easy for another, it is necessary to assess the right level of the students.

ⓐ Is the text too easy/difficult for the students?

ⓑ Is it structurally too demanding/complex?

ⓒ How much new vocabulary does it contain? Is it relevant?

④ **Presentation**: 텍스트의 내용이 잘 정리돼 있고, 공간과 여백을 적절하게 활용해야 하며, 학습을 향상시킬 수 있는 삽화를 포함해야 한다. 또한, 자료와 내용이 학생들이 읽고 싶을 정도로 잘 정리된 방식으로 설계돼야 한다.

ⓐ Does it "look" authentic?

ⓑ Is it "attractive"?

ⓒ Does it grab the students' attention?

ⓓ Does it make him want to read more?

(2) Positive and Negative Aspects of Authentic Materials

Authentic materials는 학습자의 수준 등에 따라 긍정적인 측면과 부정적인 측면 모두 고려돼야 한다. Authentic materials는 실제 목표 문화에 대한 정보를 제공할 수 있으며, 실생활에서 사용되는 언어에 노출될 수 있고, 학습자의 요구에 민감한 읽기가 진행될 수 있다는 장점이 있다. 하지만 무슨 자료를 선택하느냐에 따라, 읽기 중 학생들의 해당 문화적 지식이 없고 이해가 어려울 정도의 집약된 목표 문화가 담긴 경우가 있을 수 있으며, 특히나 low level 학생들이 언어적 어려움을 느낄 정도의 복잡한 문장 구조나 불필요하게 어려운 어휘 등이 포함된 경우도 있을 수 있다.

① **Positive aspects**: One of main ideas of using authentic materials in the classroom is to "expose" the learner to as much real language as possible.
  ⓐ Giving authentic cultural information
  ⓑ Having a positive effect on student motivation
  ⓒ Relating more closely to students' needs
  ⓓ Supporting a more creative approach to teaching

② **Negative aspects**: In authentic texts, the vocabulary may not be relevant to the learners' needs and too many structures can create difficulty. This can have the opposite effect: rather than motivate the learner, it can de-motivate—it means "...put up the affective filter."
  ⓐ Being too culturally biased (often a good knowledge of cultural background is required when reading)
  ⓑ Having too many structures being mixed, causing lower levels problems when decoding the texts
  ⓒ Containing difficult language, unneeded vocabulary items and complex language structures

Therefore, authentic materials should be used in accordance with students' ability, with suitable tasks being given in which total understanding is not important.

③ How can teachers overcome the problems created by difficult authentic text in class?
  ⓐ **Pre-reading**: Compensate for linguistic/socio-cultural inadequacies but also used to activate existing schemata
  ⓑ **While-reading**: Encourage the learner to be a flexible and active reader, promote a dialogue between reader and writer, and ask him or her to use appropriate reading strategies and switch top-down and bottom-up processing depending on the reading purpose
  ⓒ **Post-reading**: Provide a learner level-appropriate integrative tasks and further information relevant to what they learnt from reading text

Authentic materials 사용 시 text를 단순화하기보다는 읽기 전 활동으로 text에 관련한 학습자의 기초 지식을 이끌어 내거나 읽기 이해에 필요한 어휘 지도 및 학습자 능력에 맞는 과업 등을 수행해 나가도록 한다.

When you come down to it, rather than just simplifying the text by changing its language, it can be made more approachable by eliciting students' existing knowledge in pre-reading discussion, reviewing new vocabulary before reading, and then asking students to perform tasks that are within their competence, such as skimming to get the main idea or scanning for specific information, before they begin intensive reading.

2 Lesson Procedure

(1) Pre-reading

본격적인 읽기 활동 전에 일정 시간을 할애해 글의 주제를 소개함으로써 스키마를 활성화하고 동기를 부여한다.

This stage is to prepare students for what they are going to read, just as we are usually prepared in real life.

① 목적

ⓐ To <u>motivate</u> the learners to want to read the text

ⓑ To generate the <u>learners' schemata</u>

ⓒ To provide <u>any language preparation</u> that might be needed for coping with the text

② 활동

ⓐ Guess the topic of the text from the headings, illustrations

ⓑ Brainstorm around a topic word on the board

ⓒ Predict what the text will say

ⓓ Write questions that may be answered by the text (pre-set questions)

Plus ⊕

Brainstorming & Semantic Mapping

One very popular kind of pre-reading task is "brainstorming." This may take the form of giving the class a particular key word or key concept, or it may be a newspaper headline or book title. Students are then invited to call out words and concepts they personally associate with the key word or words provided by the teacher.

Brainstorming has many advantages as a classroom procedure. First, it requires little teacher preparation; second, it allows learners considerable freedom to bring their own prior knowledge and opinions to bear on a particular issue, and third, it can involve the whole class. No one needs feel threatened when any bid is acceptable and can be added to the framework. For example, these are the kinds of associations which might be called up by the key word, 'environmental pollution': "water pollution," "air pollution," "global warming," "melting ice," "getting higher the sea temperature."

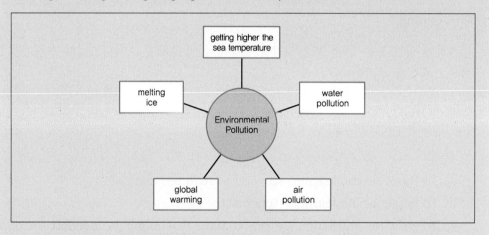

These bids reflect very different categories and level of generalization. However, the initial random associations can be classified and subcategorized either by the teacher or the students, and additional contribution from class members or the teacher added to 'stretch' existing concepts. The results of this kind of activity resemble what has been called 'semantic mapping.'

> ▶ **Semantic mapping**: 제시된 지문을 읽을 때 여러 가지 사건이나 생각을 관련 항목끼리 묶어 보거나 의미론적 지도를 그려보는 전략이다.
>
> The strategy of semantic mapping, or grouping ideas into meaningful clusters, helps the students to provide some order to the chaos. Also, students use this strategy to collaboratively induce order or hierarchy of a passage.

(2) While-reading

읽기 과업을 바탕으로 특정 사실이나 수사적 장치 등에 주목해 텍스트를 읽도록 한다. 읽기 과업은 학습자들에게 일종의 목적의식을 가지고 글을 읽도록 한다.

This stage is to help the learners understand the text. They may first do an easy scanning or skimming task, and then a task requiring more thorough comprehension. As with listening, teachers should help students understand the text rather than just testing their comprehension the whole time.

① 목적
    ⓐ To enable learners to confirm predictions made during pre-reading
    ⓑ To help students to understand the specific content
    ⓒ To perceive the rhetorical structure of the text

② 활동
    ⓐ Skim for the general idea
    ⓑ Scan two to four pieces of information
    ⓒ Answer questions and complete sentences or a table
    ⓓ Ask each other questions

In the Classroom

Reading Activity Examples

1. Identify topic sentence and main idea of paragraphs.

> ▶ Skimming: 텍스트의 전반적인 내용, 전체 구조, 중심 내용 등을 알아내기 위해 텍스트 전체를 재빨리 읽는 전략이다.

2. Distinguish between general and specific ideas.

> **Ex**
> • To save the earth we should recycle wastes properly.
> • We should rinse off the finished drinks.

3. Identify the connectors: to see how they link ideas within the text.

Transitions provide <u>greater cohesion</u> by making it more explicit or signaling how ideas relate to one another.

> **Ex**
> Many students don't rinse off their finished drinks. *However*, we don't forget to rinse them off before you recycle your finished drinks. *In addition*, we do not remove the label on the plastic bottles.

4. Answer literal and inferential questions.

'Literal' simply refers to what the text says and 'inferential' is using the text as a starting point to get a deeper meaning.

> ▶ Literal comprehension level
> 텍스트에 명시적으로 제시된 내용에 대한 이해이다.
>
> Answers are directly and explicitly expressed in the text. Students can answer in the words of the text.
>
> ▶ Inferential (interpretive) level: reading between the lines
> 명시적인 의미 이외에 숨겨진 의미(intended meaning)를 파악, 추론하는 단계이다.
> The students consider what is implied but not explicitly stated. The readers may put together pieces of information that are scattered throughout the text.

► Evaluative (critical) level: personal judgement

작가의 의도나 주장에 대해서 독자가 개인적으로 판단, 평가하는 단계이다. 즉, 읽은 글을 맹목적으로 수용하는 대신, 글의 내용에 담긴 가치관과 글의 수준 및 사실의 정확성까지도 일일이 따져가면서 평가하는 단계이다.

The students considerately judge the text in terms of what the writer is trying to do and how far she has achieved it. The reader may be asked to judge ① the writer's honesty or bias, ② the force of her argument, and ③ the effectiveness of her narrative power.

5. Infer the meaning of new words using the context.

► Guessing strategy

모르는 단어나 어려운 문장이 나올 경우 배경지식이나 텍스트에 나와 있는 단서를 통해 단어 혹은 문장의 의미를 추측하는 전략이다. 단, 교사는 학생들의 추측을 장려하되 최대한 정확한 추측(accurate guesses)을 하는 방법을 지도한다.

► Inferencing strategy

Inferring—making inferences—is often described as making a logical guess or 'reading between the lines'. Readers make inferences when they are able to take their own experiences and combine them with information they gather from what they read. The result is that they create new meaning or draw conclusion that isn't explicitly stated in the reading.

6. Student-to-student conversation

Students have a conversation after they have finished a paragraph so they can clear up any confusions they might have.

7. Scan a text for a specific information.

Students scan when they look for their favorite show listed in the TV guides, when they took their friend's phone number in their contact list.

► Scanning: 텍스트에 나와 있는 특정 정보(names, prices, dates, etc)를 찾기 위해 텍스트를 재빨리 읽는 전략이다.

 **In the Classroom**

Comprehension Level of Questions

Text 1: **A Son to Be Proud of**

Last week, Rahman's wife Leila had an accident. Rahman's youngest child, Yusof, was at home when it happened. He was playing with his new toy car. Rahman had given it to him the week before, for his third birthday.

Suddenly Yusof heard his mother calling 'Help! Help!' He ran to the kitchen. His mother had burned herself with some hot cooking oil. She was crying with pain and the pan was on fire.

Rahman had gone to his office. Both the other children had gone to school. Yusof was too small to help his mother, and she was too frightened to speak sensibly to him. But he ran to the neighbor's house and asked her to come and help his mother. She soon put out the fire and took Yusof's mother to the clinic.

When Rahman came home, Leila told him what had happened. He was very proud of his son. 'When you are a man, you will be just like your father,' he said.

---

1. Questions of Literal Comprehension

   • What accident did Leila have?
   • What was Yusof doing when the accident happened?

2. Questions of Reorganization (or reinterpretation)

   • How old was Yusof? (Reinterpret third birthday, the week before)
   • How many children did Rahman have? (Reorganize: 1[Yusof]+2[Both the other children]=3)

3. Questions of Inference

   Why was Rahman proud of his son?

01

Text 2

Gregory is about forty-five and his hair is starting to go grey. Everybody knows Gregory because he reads the news on television. He has done this for ten years and enjoys it very much. He likes it when people stop him in the street or when they point at him and whisper to their friends. Yesterday his boss suggested Gregory change his job. Gregory knows his boss wants a younger man to take his place and doesn't care what happens to Gregory. The new job could never be as good as his old one. He has no one to discuss the problem with at home and this makes it worse.

4. Evaluative (critical level) Questions

- To what extent does the passage lead one to believe that television work is a 'cut-throat' type of profession with little regard for personal feelings or loyalty?
- Popular appeal is more important than professional ability in a competitive situation where different television companies are struggling for supremacy.

TRUE □   FALSE □

---

(3) Post-reading

읽기 지문에 대한 질문 제시와 글의 목적 및 전개 방식 등에 대한 토론, 어휘/문법적 구조에 대한 확장 학습, 해당 지문과 연관된 쓰기 활동 등의 통합식 수업 등으로 진행할 수 있다.

This stage is to help students to connect what they have read with their own ideas and experience, just as we often do in real life, and perhaps to move fluently from reading to another classroom activity.

① 목적

ⓐ To review the content working on bottom-up concerns such as grammar, vocabulary, and discourse features

ⓑ To give learners further practice using the content of the text; to further check understanding of the text through another medium

ⓒ To integrate the new information from the text with what the students already know

② 활동

ⓐ Discuss what was interesting or new in the text

ⓑ Discuss or debate the topic of the text if it is controversial

ⓒ Do tasks on the language of structure of the text

ⓓ Summarize the text either orally or in writing

(4) Example of a Lesson Plan

Classroom Condition	Middle school, 3rd grade, 24 students, mixed-level, block-time class (90 mins.)
Lesson Objectives	• Students will be able to identify detailed information from the reading text. • Students will be able to do a survey on recycling behavior of the classmates. • Students will be able to write their suggestions.
Unit	Environmental Awareness
Title	Small Actions for the Earth
Periods	3-4/8 periods (reading, speaking, writing)

• Reading Material •

Let's Recycle Properly!

Hi, my name is Jiho. I am a president of our school green club, "The Green Avengers." In our club, we studied how to recycle waste effectively. Recycling in our school is not done properly, so I'd like to suggest the right ways to recycle properly. First, many students don't rinse off their finished drinks. Don't forget to rinse them off before you recycle your finished drinks. Second, students do not remove the label on the plastic bottles. Make sure you remove the labels before recycling the plastic bottles. Third, stained paper such as pizza boxes is not recyclable. Do not put such items in the recycling bin. Fourth, many students put recycling items such as plastic bottles, and waste papers in the garbage. Please do not put such items in the garbage. Your small actions can make big changes and help the Earth.

• While-reading Activity •

	Problem	Suggestion
1		
2		
3		
4		

• Post-reading Activity 1. Speaking Task : Survey •

	Never	Seldom	Often	Always
1. Do you put recycling items such as plastic bottles in a recycling bin?	⦀⦀			
2. Do you rinse off the drinks before you put them in the recycling bin?				
3. Do you remove the labels of the plastic bottles?				
4. (Your own sentence)				

• Post-reading Activity 2. Writing Task •

Our group's suggestion for better recycling

We think the most serious problem in our school's recycling is that _____

_____

because _____

_____ .

We should _____

_____ .

• The Sample of Lesson Procedure •

Teacher	Students
T shows a video clip on the topic "Save the earth" and asks Ss brainstorm the topic.	Ss watch the video clip and talk about their ideas related to the topic.
T asks Ss to read Material 1 and find out the main idea.	Ss read Material 1 individually and find out the main idea.
T presents three underlined words in context and instructs one of these words. • recyclable: Paper, bottles and glass can be reused and recyclable. • stained: I spilt milk on my blouse. That's why it got stained. • remove: I want to remove the stain from my blouse.	Ss guess the meaning of the presented three words from context. • recyclable = reused • stained • remove
Reading Activity	
T gives each pair a table in Material 2 to fill out with detailed information from Material 1. | Do's(Problem)	Don'ts (Suggestion) | |---|---| | •	• | | •	• | | •	•		In pairs, Ss read Material 1 and complete the table with detailed information from Material 1.
T asks Ss to read Material 1 again with their partner and fill out the table based on what they read.	
T pick some of pairs and have them present each Do's and Don'ts one after another.	Volunteer pairs present their DO's and Don'ts.
Based on the presentation, T summarize what to do for the earth.	
Speaking Activity	
T makes students into a group of 4 and distributes a survey table to each group.	

T reads the first column and demonstrates how to do a survey by asking Ss to raise their hands if they have done so.	Ss listen to the first column and express how they have done for the earth by a show of hands.
T asks Ss to add their own ideas to survey lists.	Ss call out their own ideas.
T asks Ss to decide their role in groups and leads them to do a survey.	
Walking around the classroom T provides Ss with language help if needed.	
T provides some feedback on content and language. • Content: *remove the labels of plastic bottles before throwing into **a recycling bin not a trash bin**.* • Language: *rinse **of** → rinse **off***	
Writing Activity	
T presents Material 4 on OHP and asks Ss to write their group suggestions based on Material 4.	Ss look at Material 4.
T shows a model writing and asks Ss to read it aloud. **Model writing: Our group suggestions for better recycling** Our group thinks the most serious problem in our school is that most of students do not rinse off the finished drinks because it's such a bother. Therefore, we should rinse off the finished drinks before throwing them into a recycling bin.	Ss read T's model writing and read it aloud.
T asks Ss to write the group suggestion based on the survey result in 5 minutes.	
T asks Ss to post their own group suggestion to the class blog by 7 p.m.	

3 Extensive Reading and Intensive Reading

읽기 활동은 다양한 읽기 목적에 따라 이뤄지며, 특히 읽기는 주요 3가지 목적인 실생활 읽기(for survival), 학습을 위한 읽기(intensive), 즐거움 및 다독을 위한 읽기(extensive)를 토대로 진행된다.

The reason for reading depends very much on the purpose for reading. Reading can have three main purposes, for survival, for learning, for pleasure. Reading for survival is considered to be in response to our environment, to find out information and can include street signs, advertising, and timetables. It depends very much on the day-to-day needs of the reader, and often involves an immediate response to a situation. In contrast reading for learning is considered to be the type of reading done in the classroom and is goal-oriented. Reading for pleasure includes the following central ideas:

① The idea of meaning

② The transfer of meaning from one mind to another

③ The transfer of a message from writer to reader

④ How we get meaning by reading

⑤ How the reader, the writer and the text all contribute to the process

(1) Extensive Reading

다양한 텍스트 혹은 보다 긴 텍스트를 즐거움과 전반적인 내용 이해를 위한 읽기 활동으로 대부분 교실 밖의 실생활(real-life)에서 이뤄진다.

① It means reading many books or longer text without a focus on classroom exercises.
② It does not aim to test comprehension skills.
③ The teacher encourages students to choose for themselves what they read and to do so for pleasure and general language improvement.
④ Read the text fluently and fast for entertainment and general understanding but without such careful attention to the details.
⑤ The more someone read, the more they pick up vocabulary and grammar from the texts without realizing it.

(2) Intensive Reading

특정 텍스트의 정확한 이해 혹은 읽기 기능 연습을 위해 교실 수업에서 행해지는 읽기 활동이다.

① It involves textbook activities to develop comprehension or a particular reading skill.
② Read the texts closely and carefully with the intention of gaining an understanding of as much detail as possible.

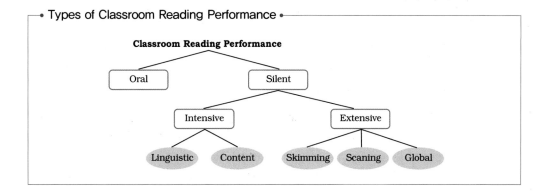

• Types of Classroom Reading Performance •

③ Jigsaw Reading

 **In the Classroom** ||||||||||||||||||||||||||||||||||||||||||||||||||||||||||||||||||||||||||||||||||||||||||||||||||||

Sample Reading Lesson

1. Pre-reading

Task 1. Teacher asks class these questions:

T: Where is Liberia?

Who can find it on this map?

Do you know anyone from Liberia or another country in Africa?

Task 2

T: Let's see how much you know about Liberia. Don't worry if you are not sure. You will read what other students wrote about this country later in the lesson.

Are these sentences true or false? Circle True or False.		
True	False	Most people in Liberia have electricity.
True	False	People speak many languages in Liberia.
True	False	Liberia is on the east coast of Africa.
True	False	Many people buy and sell food at the market.
True	False	Liberia was named by slaves who returned to Africa.

Compare your answers with partners.

2. Reading Activities

The reading on Liberia with the multiple sections makes it ideal for the technique called jigsaw reading.

T: Now you can learn more about Liberia. Some of you will learn food, some about people and some about the history.

Three groups (A, B, and C) are created and each one is given only one section of the reading about Liberia (A: People, B: History, C: Food). Each group (A group, B group, C group) is given the worksheet below and must work together to find answers to only their questions.

Work with your group to find answers to these questions.

Group A: People	• How do people make money? • Where do they get clothing? • What languages do they speak? • How is life in Monrovia?
Group B: History	• Where is Liberia? • How was it named? • What is the capital?
Group C: Food	• What do people eat in the morning? • What do people eat for lunch and dinner? • What foods grow in Liberia?

Once each group has answered the questions for their section, the teacher creates new groups made up of one member from each of the original groups (ABC, ABC, etc). Students in the new groups present the information found in their section on People, History, or Food.

As students listen to their classmates, they write answers to the questions for the sections they did not read.

T: Now go back to the true and false questions to see if your guesses were correct.

3. Follow-up / Post-reading

Now interview your classmates to learn some things about the history, people, and foods from their countries. Use the same questions you used for the reading activity.

	People	History	Food
Country			
Country			
Country			

④ Language Experience Approach(LEA)

 **In the Classroom** ||||||||||||||||||||||||||||||||||||||||||||||||||||||||||||||||||||||||||||||||||||||||||||||||

Classroom Example of Language Experience Approach

Stage 1

The students of class dictate a "story" usually based upon an experience they have had, that the teacher writes down on a large sheet of paper. The teacher tries to maintain the extra wording and expressions that the students have dictated (if it contains errors, the students can correct them later as their proficiency increases).

Stage 2

The teacher then either reads the story to the class (if the students are beginning readers), or has the class read back the story they have composed, providing any help they need along the way to figure out individual words.

Stage 3

Depending on their level of ability and needs, the class will then engage in various extended activities based upon the original story, including focusing on individual words, letters or meanings of various noteworthy parts.

Stage 4

Ultimately, the students are expected to move from the stories they have dictated toward being able to read those written by others.

Plus ➕

The Condition of Text

1. Cohesion

글의 결합력을 보여주는 장치들로서 문법적인 요소와 관련돼 표면적으로 파악이 가능하다.

① Grammatical cohesion
- Reference : 반복되는 단어 사용을 피하기 위해 사용되는 인칭대명사(pronouns), 지시대명사(demonstratives), 정관사(definite article) 등이 포함된다.
- Ellipsis : 반복되는 단어나 구문 중 문맥을 통해서 독자가 충분히 예측 가능한 구분은 생략한다.
- Substitution : 생략과 함께 생략된 단어, 구 등을 do so, one 등으로 대체한다.
- Conjunction : 한 문장과 다른 한 문장 간의 관계를 보여주는 접속사가 포함된다.

Categories		Examples
Reference	Personal	"I just met your brother. He's a nice guy."
	Demonstrative	"You failed the test. This is bad news."
	Comparative	"I asked for this bag. But I got the other bag."
Substitution and Ellipsis*	Nominal	"Can I have another drink? This one is finished."
	Verbal	"You look great." "So do you."
	Clausal	"Is she happy?" "I think so."
Conjunction	Adversative	"I didn't study. However, I still passed."
	Additive	"He didn't study. And he failed."
	Temporal	"She studied hard. Then she passed the test."
	Causal	"They studied hard. Therefore they deserve to pass."

*The examples illustrate substitution

② Lexical cohesion
- Reiteration : 앞에서 나온 단어를 생략이나 대체 없이 반복해서 쓴다.

  Ex ┊ Hand me the book. That book on the table.

- Collocation : 제시된 단어와 함께 쓰일 수 있는 단어를 사용한다.

  Ex ┊ The book arrived in the mail. The cover was ripped off and the pages were torn.

- **Superordinate**: 해당 단어보다 상위 개념을 사용해 단어의 반복을 피한다.

  Ex There are <u>roses</u> in the garden. He loves to water the <u>flower</u>.

- **General words**: stuff, thing 등의 일반적인 단어를 사용하는 경우가 해당된다.

  Ex Give me the <u>box</u>. No, the <u>thing</u> on your right side.

2. Coherence

글의 기능적 연결과 통일성을 보여주는 요소로서 표면적으로 드러나 있지 않고 의미를 통해 파악이 가능하다.

Coherence means the utterances in a text go together even though there are no explicit cohesive links between the utterances.

Ex A: That's the telephone.

B: I'm in the bath.

A: Okay.

위의 대화는 표면적인 결합장치가 없지만 발화의 의도된 의미(intended meaning)가 기능적인 연결을 이루면서 대화 전체가 하나의 통일된 상황을 보여준다.

Chapter
02

Productive Skills

Chapter
02

Productive Skills

01 \ Teaching Speaking

말하기(speaking)란 '다양한 맥락 안에서 언어 또는 비언어적 수단을 통해 서로의 생각을 나누는 과정'이다. 따라서 외국어 교수 및 학습에서 말하기란 매우 중요한 부분으로 간주된다. 하지만 이런 중요성에도 불구하고 대부분의 전통적인 교실 수업에서는 말하기가 반복 연습의 형태(a repetition of drills)나 대화 암기(memorization of dialogue)에 그치고 말았다. 이에 현재 교실 수업의 방향은 각기 다른 의사소통 상황에서 학생들이 자신의 의사를 표현하고 언어가 지닌 사회적/문화적 규율을 적절히 지키고자 한다.

Speaking is "the process of building and sharing meaning through the use of verbal and non-verbal symbols, in a variety of contexts". (Chaney, 1998, p. 13)

1 How To Teach Speaking

현재 교실 수업에서 가장 효과적인 말하기 수업은 의사소통 언어교수(communicative language teaching)와 협력학습(collaborative learning)을 토대로 학생들 간의 상호작용을 기반(interaction-based language teaching)으로 하는 수업이다.

Communicative language teaching is based on real-life situations that require communication. By using this method in ESL classes, students will have the opportunity of communicating with each other in the target language. In brief, ESL teachers should create a classroom environment where students have real-life communication, authentic activities, and meaningful tasks that promote oral language. This can occur when students collaborate in groups to achieve a goal or to complete a task.

(1) Plan speaking tasks that involve negotiation for meaning.

학습자들이 자신의 언어를 더 발전시키고 연습할 수 있는 기회를 가질 수 있도록 의미 협상이 수반되는 말하기 활동을 계획한다.

In the process of negotiation for meaning, the language addressed to learners gets adjusted to their level and becomes comprehensible to them: it provides *comprehensible input*. And as learners work to make themselves understood, they must attend to accuracy: it helps students create *comprehensible output*. This is, they are asked to select the right vocabulary, apply grammar rules and pronounce words carefully whenever students use incorrect forms. Accordingly, by planning speaking tasks that require learners to negotiate for meaning, teachers should give students valuable chances for practice and language development.

① **Discussion**: Before the discussion, it is essential that the purpose of the discussion activity is set by the teacher. In this way, the discussion points are relevant to this purpose, so that students do not spend their time chatting with each other about irrelevant things.

ⓐ Students can become involved in agree/disagree discussions.

ⓑ The teacher can form groups of students, preferably 4 or 5 in each group.

ⓒ The teacher provides controversial sentences like *"people learn best when they read vs. people learn best when they travel."*

ⓓ Each group works on their topic for a given time period, and presents their opinions to the class.

ⓔ It is essential that the speaking should be equally divided among group members. (equal turn-taking)

Discussion에 참여하는 학생들은 critical thinking이나 quick decision making을 하게 되며, 반대 의견에 대한 자신의 의사를 정중하고(in polite ways) 타당하게 제시할 수 있는 방법을 습득하게 된다. 또한, 모든 discussions 활동에서 학생들은 질문하고(to ask questions), 생각을 다시 한 번 표현해 보고(to paraphrase ideas), 자신의 생각에 대한 근거를 대고(to express support), 상대에게 세부 설명에 대한 점검(to check for clarification)을 하도록 해야 한다.

② **Role-play**: Role-play는 학생들이 다양한 사회적 맥락 안에서 여러 가지 사회적 역할을 수행하면서 의사소통에 참여하는 활동이다.

In role-play activities, the teacher gives information to the learners such as *who they are* and *what they think or feel*. Thus, the teacher can tell the student that "You are David, you go to the doctor and tell him what happened last night, and…" (Harmer, 1984)

③ **Simulations**: Simulations는 role-play와 유사하지만, role-play보다 정교하고 섬세하게 진행되는 활동이다. 즉, simulations에서는 실제 환경(realistic environment)을 만들기 위해 필요한 실제 items를 교실로 가져오는데, 가령, 학생의 역할이 'singer'일 경우 'a microphone'을 가져온다. Role-play와 simulation의 장점은 학생들이 즐겁게 과업에 참여할 수 있으므로 동기유발이 되며, 특히나 상이한 역할로 인해 각자의 과업에 대한 책임감이 다르므로 hesitant students의 경우 다른 활동에 비해 본인의 부담이 적어 자신감을 갖고 활동에 참여할 수 있다.

Role plays and simulations have many advantages. First, since they are entertaining, they motivate the students. Second, as Harmer (1984) suggests, they increase the self-confidence of hesitant students, because in role play and simulation activities, they will have a different role and do not have to speak for themselves, which means they do not have to take the same responsibility.

④ **Information Gap**: 대부분 pairwork으로 진행되며, 한 명이 정보를 가지고 있으면, 해당 정보를 필요로 하는 다른 한 명으로 인해 정보를 얻기 위한 의사소통 활동이 필연적으로 일어난다. Information gap 활동은 group work으로 진행될 경우 jigsaw 활동 등으로 확장될 수 있다.

In this activity, students are supposed to be working in pairs. One student will have the information that the other partner does not have and the partners will share their information. Information gap activities serve many purposes such as solving a problem or collecting information. Also, each partner plays an important role because the task cannot be completed if the partners do not provide the information the others need. These activities are effective because everybody has the opportunity to talk extensively in the target language.

⑤ Jigsaw: 기본적인 jigsaw 활동은 각각 다른 정보를 가진 4~5명의 학생들로 구성된 채 진행되며, group member 간의 information gap이 존재하므로 각각 가지고 있는 정보를 공유하면서 주어진 과업을 완성해 나가도록 한다.

Example

You Are a Witness!

1. The teacher prepares a set of four picture cards showing the story of a minor car accident. She divides the class into four groups, with four students in each group. She tells the class that they are going to witness a car accident, but that they can see only one card.

2. The teacher flashes one picture card to each group for a few seconds only. Then she asks the members of each group to discuss and agree on what they have just seen.

3. The teacher assigns each member of each group a number: 1, 2, 3, and 4. Then she re-groups students as follows:

| 1234 | 1234 | 1234 | 1234 | ⇨ | 1111 | 2222 | 3333 | 4444 |

4. The teacher asks the members of the new groups to describe what each person has seen and to decide on the sequence of the accident.

⑥ Brainstorming: 주어진 topic을 토대로 제한 시간 안에 topic과 관련된 생각을 자유롭게 이끌어 내는 활동으로, 참여하는 모든 학생들이 topic에 대한 새로운 생각을 공유할 수 있으며 topic에 대한 기존의 schematic knowledge 등을 활성화할 수 있다.

On a given topic, students can produce ideas in a limited time. Depending on the context, either individual or group brainstorming is effective and learners generate ideas quickly and freely. The good characteristics of brainstorming is that the students are not criticized for their ideas so students will be open to sharing new ideas.

⑦ Storytelling: Storytelling은 들은 이야기를 다시 요약하거나, 새로운 이야기를 만들어 말하는 활동으로, 이 활동에 참여하는 모든 학생들은 이야기가 갖고 있어야 하는 character와 setting을 포함해 이야기의 시작, 전개 및 끝맺음의 format으로 자신의 생각과 이야기를 표현해 볼 수 있다.

Students can briefly summarize a tale or story they heard from somebody beforehand, or they may create their own stories to tell their classmates. Storytelling fosters creative thinking. It also helps students express ideas in the format of beginning, development, and ending, including the characters and setting a story has to have. Students also can tell riddles or jokes. For instance, at the very beginning of each class session, the teacher may call a few students to tell short riddles or jokes as an opening. In this way, not only will the teacher address students' speaking ability, but also get the attention of the class. Another version is a story completion activity. This is a very enjoyable, whole-class and free-speaking activity for which students sit in a circle. For this activity, a teacher starts to tell a story, but after a few sentences he or she stops narrating. Then, each student starts to narrate from the point where the previous one stopped. Each student is supposed to add from four to ten sentences.

⑧ **Picture Narrating / Picture Describing:** 학생들의 oral skills을 키우기 위해 그림을 이용해 진행하는 대표적인 활동이다. Picture narrating은 학생들에게 몇 장의 연속된 그림을 제공해 그림 속에 펼쳐지는 이야기를 말해 보도록 하는 활동이며, picture describing은 group별로 다른 그림을 제공해 그림 안에서 일어나는 일을 묘사해 보도록 하는 활동이다. 이와 같은 활동을 하기 전, 교사는 학생들에게 rubrics를 제공해 학생들이 주의해야 할 평가 기준에 주의를 기울이며 말하기 활동에 참여하도록 하는 것이 효과적이다. 특히, rubrics 안에는 과제를 수행할 때 필요한 어휘나 언어 구조에 대한 요소가 포함돼야 한다.

Picture narrating is based on several sequential pictures. Students are asked to tell the story taking place in the sequential pictures by paying attention to the criteria provided by the teacher as a rubric. Rubrics can include the vocabulary or structures they need to use while narrating. Picture describing, another way to make use of pictures in a speaking activity is to give students just one picture and having them describe what it is in the picture. For this activity students can form groups and each group is given a different picture. Students discuss the picture with their groups, then a spokesperson for each group describes the picture to the whole class. This activity fosters the creativity and imagination of the learners as well as their public speaking skills.

⑨ **Find the Difference**: 짝끼리 진행하는 활동으로 각자에게 서로 다른 그림을 제공해 그림에서 찾을 수 있는 차이점과 비슷한 점을 토대로 정보를 나눠 보도록 하는 활동이다(information exchange activity).

For this activity students can work in pairs and each couple is given two different pictures, for example, picture of boys playing football and another picture of girls playing tennis. Students in pairs discuss the similarities and/or differences in the pictures.

(2) **Personalize the content of speaking activities whenever possible.**

학습자들이 각자의 환경, 흥미, 목표 등을 활용해 말할 수 있는 활동을 계획한다. 학생들이 참여하는 활동은 학생들이 중심이 돼 자신의 생각이나 기호(preference), 필요 등이 말하기 내용에 담기도록 하는 것이 효과적이다. 가령, 학생들에 의한 topic 선정, 학생들의 흥미와 관심에 초점을 둔 reading passages나 말하기 과업 등을 진행한다.

Personalisation happens when activities allow students to use language to express their own ideas, feelings, preferences and opinions. Personalisation is an important part of the communicative approach, since it involves true communication, as learners communicate real information about themselves. For example, students have read a text about sports. In pairs they talk about what their favourite sports are and whether they prefer to play or watch. In the classroom personalisation is important for several reasons. It makes language relevant to learners, makes communication activities meaningful, and also helps memorisation. Personalisation can take place at any stage of a lesson.

(3) **Provide opportunities for learners to notice the gap.**

말하기 활동을 토대로 학생들은 '자신이 말하고 싶은 것'과 '말할 수 있는 것'의 차이를 인식할 수 있다. 이 차이에 대한 인식을 토대로 학습과 언어 발달이 일어난다.

What does it mean to say that learners should be given opportunities to "notice the gap?" This phrase describes an experience that learners have when they are interacting in English. It refers to the learner realizing that the way she is saying something in the target language differs from the way native or proficient speakers say it. This awareness can be about individual words, grammar rules, idioms, appropriate phrases, pronunciation—any component of the language she is learning. Some researchers believe that this awareness must occur before a learner can make the necessary adjustments in her developing competence.

> ▶ The ideas of noticing the gap is not the same as *monitoring* one's own output. The concept of monitoring refers to learners checking what they say or write, based on rules they've already learned. Monitoring may lead learners to notice the gap, but this experience can happen in the absence of known rules.

Noticing the gap can involve the learner's realization that she doesn't know the word or the structure she is trying to say. In fact, the phrase "noticing the gap" has also been used with the idea of learners realizing that there are differences between what they want to say and what they can say. This process involves the development of linguistic self-awareness on the learners' part.

(4) Balance a focus on accuracy with focus on fluency as well.

영어 수행력은 영어의 유창성과 정확성을 모두 일컫는 것으로, 교실 수업에서는 학생들의 의사소통 능력을 극대화할 수 있는 언어 사용을 위한 meaning-focused activities와 의사소통의 정확성을 길러 나갈 수 있는 form-focused activities를 함께 다뤄야 할 것이다.

Teachers encourage students to use natural language which is likely to take place when speaking activities focus on meaning and its negotiation, when speaking strategies are used, and when overt correction is minimized. While fluency may in many communicative language courses be an initial goal in language teaching, accuracy is achieved to some extent by allowing students to focus on the elements of phonology, grammar, and discourse in their spoken output.

① **Task-based instruction**: 과제 기반 수업은 학습자에게 의미와 유창성을 길러 나가 도록 하는 수업 모형이지만 과업 후 진행되는 언어 형태에 대한 정확성도 길러 나간 다는 측면에서 의사소통 교수의 주요 원리인 fluency와 accuracy를 함께 키워줄 수 있는 수업 모형이다.

② **Communication task types**

ⓐ **Prabhu의 분류**

• **Information-gap activity**: 정보를 가지고 있는 한 사람이 다른 사람에게 정보를 전달해 주거나 정보의 형태를 바꾸는 활동이다. 단순한 정보 진달로 싱호작용이 제한돼 있는 것이 특징이다.

Information-gap activity involves a transfer of given information from one person to another—or from one form to another, or from one place to another. One example is pair work in which each member of the pair has a part of the total information (for example an incomplete picture) and attempts to convey it verbally to the other.

• **Opinion-gap activity**: 주어진 상황에 대해 개인적인 기호나 느낌, 태도 등을 밝 히는 활동이다. 주로 토론이나 논쟁에서 쓰이며, 학습자가 어느 정도의 복잡한 언어 형태를 사용할 수 있어야 하므로 EFL 상황에서는 한계가 있다.

Opinion-gap activity involves identifying and articulating a personal preference, feeling, or attitude in response to a given situation. One example is story completion; another is taking part in the discussion of a social issue. The activity may involve using factual information and formulating arguments to justify one's opinion, but there is no objective procedure for demonstrating outcomes as right or wrong, and no reason to expect the same outcome from different individuals or on different occasions.

• **Reasoning-gap activity**: 주어진 정보를 토대로 추론, 연역적 방법, 관련성이나 형태에 대한 인식 등을 통해 새로운 정보를 도출하는 활동이다. 하나의 결과물을 위해 긴밀한 상호작용과 그룹 구성원과의 활발한 정보 교류를 촉진하기 때문에 언어 발달에 효과적이다.

Reasoning-gap activity involves driving some new information from given information through processes of inference, deduction, practical reasoning, or a perception of relationships or patterns. One example is deciding what course of action is best (for example cheapest or quickest) for a given purpose and within given constraint. The activity necessarily involves comprehending and conveying information, as an information-gap activity, but the information to be conveyed is not identical with the initially comprehended. There is a piece of reasoning which connects the two.

ⓑ Richards의 분류
- **Jigsaw tasks**: 각각 다른 정보의 조각을 하나로 합쳐 전체를 만드는 활동이다.

  Ex 전체 이야기를 세 부분으로 나누고, 3명의 학습자가 서로 다른 부분을 맡아 하나의 이야기로 만드는 활동

- **Information-gap tasks**: 한 명의 학생이 일부 정보를, 다른 학생이 상보적인 정보를 갖고 서로 상호작용을 통해 상대방의 정보가 무엇인지 찾아내는 활동이다.

- **Problem-solving tasks**: 특정 문제와 정보를 가진 학생들이 이를 해결하기 위한 해결책에 도달하는 활동으로, 일반적으로 하나의 해결책이 도출된다.

- **Decision-making tasks**: 학생들이 주어진 문제에 대한 여러 가지 대안 중 협상과 토론을 통해 한 가지를 선택하는 활동이다.

- **Opinion exchange tasks**: 토론에 참여한 학생들이 각자의 생각을 교환하는 활동으로, 하나의 결론에 도달해야 할 필요는 없다.

• Task Types •

	Interactant relationship	Interaction requirement	Goal orientation	Outcome options
Jigsaw	two-way	required	convergent	closed
Information gap	one-way or two-way	required	convergent	closed
Problem solving	one-way or two-way	optional	convergent	closed
Decision making	one-way or two-way	optional	convergent	open
Opinion exchange	one-way or two-way	optional	divergent	open

ⓒ **Task difficulty**: 말하기 활동의 난이도와 관련해 교사가 고려해야 하는 세 가지 요소는 자료, 과업 그리고 학습자 요인이다.

Text	• How dense/complex are the texts that learners are required to process? • How abstract/concrete is the content in relation to the learners experience? • How much contextual support is provided?
Task	• How many steps are involved in the task? • How relevant and meaningful is the task? • How much time is available? • What degree of grammatical accuracy is provided? • How much practice or rehearsal time is available?
Learner	• the level of confidence • motivation of learners • prior knowledge of content • degree of linguistic knowledge • skill, extent of cultural knowledge • degree of familiarity with task type itself

ⓓ **Level-differentiated task**: Advanced level의 학생과 intermediate–low level의 학생에게 동일한 과업인 dictogloss의 활동을 제공할 경우 다음과 같이 task difficulty가 조정될 수 있다.

• Level–differentiated Task •

TASK	
Step 1	Step 1
T: I'm going to read you the passage twice. First, I'll read it at normal speed and then I'll read it again as slowly as possible. As you listen, write down as many words and phrases as possible.	T: I am going to read you the passage twice. Both times, I will read it very slowly and clearly. As you listen, write down any words you hear.
Have you ever seen the Pyramids of Egypt? Have you ever wondered why they were built and how they were built? The Pyramids were built because the kings wanted to live after they died. They thought why they would live after they died. The Pyramids were constructed on the west side of Nile River. They were built there because the sun rises in the east and sets in the west. They believed why the king and the sun god would be born and born again, just like the sun. The Pyramids were very difficult to build, but the whole world can enjoy them.	[the same passage as the one for the advanced level]

Step 2	Step 2
T: Now, in groups of three, share your notes and see whether your group can come up with its own version of the text. Once your group has reconstructed the text, check it to make sure the meaning is similar to the text you heard. Also check it carefully for grammatical mistakes.	T: Now, let's rewrite the text. First, in groups of three, put together all the words that each member heard. Then, working in your group, try to make sentences with those words. And then compare your group's sentences with other groups' sentences. Using all the sentences available, rewrite the text. And check it to make sure the meaning is similar to the text I read.
Step 3	**Step 3**
T: Now, I'll pass out the original text that I read to you. Compare your group's text with the original one. How is the original different from yours? Look at both content and passive forms. And then make a presentation about the differences you've found between the two texts.	T: Now, I will give you the original text. On the text, I've already underlined some parts. [Only the passive forms in the text are underlined.] Mark the parts in your group's text that you think match those underlined parts. Make your group's text as similar as possible to the original text.

③ **Accuracy-based activities**: 정확성에 초점을 맞춘 활동들은 학생들이 언어의 유창성과 의사소통 능력을 키우는 데 필요하다. 또한, 정확성에 초점을 둔 활동을 meaningful하게 진행할 필요가 있으며, 더 나아가 학생들이 직접 의사소통을 할 때 학습되는 target forms를 사용해 볼 기회를 제공하도록 한다.

The purpose of form-focused work in speaking activities is to equip the student with the knowledge and skills needed for communication. The first need for accuracy-based activity design is *contextualized practice*. This means finding a situation in which structure is commonly used. The second need is *to personalize the language* in activities which enable students to express their own ideas, feelings, preferences, and opinions.

Plus ⊕

Extract 1: Mechanical Drill

Mechanical drills have only one correct response from a student and have no implied connection with reality.

T : Watch–Japan. Yuri.
L1 : The watch was made in Japan.
T : Good. Shoes–Italy, Kim.
L2 : The shoes was... were made in Italy.
T : Mm... Again.
L2 : ... The shoes were made in Italy.
T : OK. Calculator–China. Joon.
L3 : The calculator was made in China.
T : Car–USA. Elena.

Extract 2: Meaningful Drill

What some have called meaningful drills can add some reality, but may stretch the concept of drill too far. And the process may continue on as the teacher reinforces certain grammatical or phonological elements, but connects utterances to reality. This is more appropriately a case of what one could call meaningful practice, useful in virtually any communicative classroom.

T : Where was the Mercedes made, Hyunsoo?
L1 : It was made in Germany.
T : Right. Where was the Ferrari made, Kim?
L2 : It made in Italy.
T : It...?
L2 : It... was... made in Italy.
T : Good. It was made in Italy. Where was the Buick made, Min?
L3 : It was made in the USA.
T : Right. Where was the Jaguar made, Joon?

Extract 3: Communicative Drill (form-focused communicative practice)

A further extension of meaningful communicative practice is found in <u>form-focused</u> <u>communicative practice</u> that might go something like this, if you were trying to get students to practice the past tense.

Case 1

T   : Good morning, class. Last weekend I went to a restaurant and ate salmon. Juan, what did you do last weekend?

Juan : I went to park and I play soccer.

T   : Juan, you play soccer or you played soccer?

Juan : Oh... eh... I played soccer.

T   : Good! Ying, did you go to the park last weekend?

Ying : No.

T   : What did you do?

Ying : I went to a movie.

T   : Great, and what did you do, Fay?

Case 2

T   : OK, check your watches, calculator, pens...

L1   : Our shoes, teacher? Our bag?

T   : Sure. Why not? OK, let's see how free trade is affecting us. What about your watch, Hyun?

L2   : My watch was made in Japan.

T   : Ah, a Citizen like mine. What about your shoes, Lucy?

L3   : They my shoes... No?... They... were made in Italy.

T   : Good. They're nice. What about your bag, Soo?

L4   : It was made in Portugal.

T   : Portugal? Really? Where was your pen made, Jung?

Comments:

세 명의 모든 교사가 학습자에게 새로운 패턴에 대한 연습으로 특정 요소를 대체하고 지속적으로 반복하도록 하고 있다. 학습자로부터 답변을 이끌어 내는 교수 기법을 모두 사용하고 있으며, 해당 연습을 통제하고 있다. 그러나 주어진 Extract마다 교사가 사용한 기법과 방식은 상당히 다르다.

Extract 1은 가장 덜 의사소통적인 연습 활동이자 object(watch, shoes, etc)와 country(Japan, Italy, etc)를 cue로 한 pattern drill 연습 활동으로 유의미성이 가장 낮다. 이에 비해 Extract 3은 교사가 target structure를 연습시키지만 학생들의 real information을 활용하고 의미에 초점을 둔 response(i.e., they're nice)를 하는 등 가장 자연스러운 의사소통을 담고 있다.

The teacher in Extract 2 uses the question pattern 'Where was the _____ made?' every time. The teacher in Extract 1 uses two-word cues (for example, 'watch-Japan') every time. The teacher in Extract 3-Case 2 uses the question pattern 'What about your _____?' several times, and then moves to the pattern 'Where was yours made?'

On a scale from unnatural/non-communicative to natural/communicative, Extracts 1, 2, and 3 might be classified something like this:

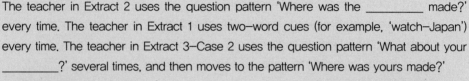

The most unnatural/non-communicative practice is in Extract 1. The teacher gets the learners to produce sentences by using the artificial cue 'object-country', for example, 'Watch-Japan.' And she does not learn any new information from the learners' answers. The most natural/communicative practice is in Extract 3. The teacher uses questions as cues, for example, 'What about your shoes' and 'Where was your pen made?' She learns real, new information from the learners' answers about where their possessions were made. And she responds with conversational comments, for example, 'They're nice.' Extract 2 comes somewhere in between. The teacher uses questions rather than cues, but there is no variation in them. The learners answer with information known to the teacher, and the teacher makes no conversational comments.

02

(5) Train students to use strategies.

학생들은 완성된 영어체계가 아닌 불완전한 영어체계(interlanguage)를 가지고 말하기 수업에 참여하기 때문에 학생들 간의 소집단 활동 시 의사소통 장애가 일어날 수 있으므로 자신의 부족한 linguistic knowledge를 극복할 수 있는 방법(communication strategies)을 배워야 한다. 따라서 교사는 실제 발생할 수 있는 의사소통 장애의 예를 제공하고 극복 방안에 대해 modelling해 주고 연습하도록 지도할 필요가 있다.

When writing as well as speaking in a second language, learners who have limited command of the second language may have to use a variety of strategies that can compensate for their lack of knowledge of the target language grammar and vocabulary in order to effectively get their intended meaning or message across to a reader or listener. Strategies employed for this purpose include **avoidance, code switching, word coinage, appeal to authority, and using prefabricated patterns**. As these strategies constitute a significant part of strategic competence, advances in the learners' ability to effectively use them play a considerable role in promoting their communicative competence.

(6) Encourage students to take responsibility for their own learning.

말하기 수업은 verbal students나 talkative students들이 turn-taking을 장악할 우려가 있으므로 반드시 학생 개개인에게 역할(individual role)이나 과업에 대한 책임(portion)을 제공해 학습 활동의 주체가 될 수 있도록 해야 하며, self-evaluation을 통해 자신의 과업에 대한 참여도 및 성과에 대한 평가를 하도록 한다.

No longer is learning seen as a one-way transfer of knowledge from teacher to student; today students learn from teacher, from classmates, and from the world outside the classroom, and the more the student seeks these opportunities, the more likely he or she will learn to use the language. In oral skills classroom, students should be allowed and encouraged to initiate communication when possible, to determine the content of their responses or contributions, and to evaluate their own production and learning progress.

(7) **Check up the levels of the students and their perceived needs.**

성공적인 말하기 수업을 진행하기 위한 선결 조건은 학생들의 수준(student level)과 학습 요구 및 필요(students' needs)에 대해 정확하게 파악하는 것이다. 따라서 교사는 다양한 channel을 통해 학생들의 요구 분석 및 필요 분석(needs analysis)을 진행해야 하며, 수업 전 학습자의 현 수준이나 학습의 출발을 파악하기 위한 placement test와 diagnostic test를 진행할 필요가 있다.

Level may be determined by a placement test or by a diagnostic test given by the teacher. Information on student needs can be obtained by means of a student information sheet on which they report the amount of time they spend speaking English, their future goals, their goals for the course, and their assessment of their overall speaking ability.

Plus ➕

Classroom Talk

1. Question Types

① **Display questions**: They seek answers in which the information is already known by the teacher. This type of elicitation has been criticised for its lack of authenticity since it is not commonly used in conversation outside the classroom. Extensive use of display questions could be a waste of time. However, it is said that display questions can potentially be central resources which language teachers and students use to organize language lessons and produce language pedagogy. Accordingly, they are an important tool in the classroom, not only for the teacher to be able to check and test their learners, but also as a source of listening practice. One of the first things a beginner learns in English is how to understand and answer display questions.

> **Ex** ⋮ The teacher asks a learner 'What is the past simple form of leave?'

② **Referential questions**: They require answers which contain information unknown by the teacher, and they are frequently used to call for evaluation or judgment. They are commonly used in regular conversation outside the classroom, hence are believed to encourage students' higher-order thinking skills and authentic use of the second language in the classroom. Many teachers agree that teachers' use of referential questions could prompt students to provide significantly longer and syntactically more complex responses than the use of display questions.

> **Ex❶** What do you think about this topic?
> What do you think about animal rights?

> **Ex❷** T: Last week we were reading "Kee Knock Stan" (title of a story). <u>What is "Kee Knock Stan,"</u> (display Q) Hyunsoo?
> S: I cannot understand.
> T: Yes.
> T: <u>What do you think the postman at the post office would do?</u> (referential Q)
> S: I think I would divide it if the letters are to Hong Kong or other places.
> T: Yes, I think that's a sensible way, right? Good.

Both questions asked by the teacher are "what" questions, but the first one is a "display" question which has only one correct answer, hence "closed." The second is a "referential" question with no pre-determined answer, hence "open."

2. Effective Questioning

효과적인 질문 기법은 학습자가 교사의 질문에 대답할 수 있도록 유도하는 것으로, 질문에 대한 대답을 이끌어 내지 못할 경우 교사는 즉각 자신의 질문을 학습자의 수준에 맞춰 수정해야 할 것이다.

Language teachers in questioning are usually to get their students to engage with the language material actively through speech; so an effective questioning technique is one that elicits fairly prompt, motivated, relevant and full responses. If, on the other hand, their questions result in long silences, or are answered by only the strongest students, or obviously bore the class, or consistently elicit only very brief or unsuccessful answers, then there is probably something wrong.

Thus, when teachers fail to elicit any response from the learners, they often need to modify their questions. There are a number of modification devices used by teachers, including <u>syntactic modifications</u> (such as making the topic salient and decomposing complex structures) and <u>semantic modifications</u> such as paraphrasing difficult words and disambiguation.

For example, in a language classroom, the teacher reads out a sentence describing a dog. She said "So that's a very good descriptive sentence. It tells you exactly what the dog looks like. Can you picture the dog?" The teacher realized that the use of the word "picture" might be a bit beyond the pupils's ability level. Therefore, she modified the question to "If I were to ask you to draw the dog, would you be able to draw the dog?" As a result of her lexical modification, the students immediately responded in chorus by saying "yes, yes."

3. Classroom Discourse

① IRE: 대부분의 교실 담화의 구조로, 다음과 같다.

> * The teacher *initiates* an assertion or asks a question.
> * The student *responds*.
> * The teacher *evaluates*, by giving an evaluative statement such as "very good" or by asking the same or similar question of another student.

IRE는 학습자들의 어휘력이나 문법적 능력의 내재화 정도를 알아보기 위해 진행되는 교실 담화 구조로, 교사가 assessing questions(한 가지 정확한 답변 및 예측 가능한 답변을 요구하는 질문)를 제시하고 학습자의 답변에 대한 평가를 'very good', 'right', 'excellent' 등으로 제공한다. 그러나 이러한 IRE의 담화는 교실 밖의 의사소통 구조를 담고 있지 않으며, 또한 의미 위주의 담화 형태로 발전해 나가지 않는다.

② IRF: 학습자의 발화에 대한 평가가 아니라, 의미 위주의 담화를 확장시켜 나가는 것에 초점을 두는 구조이다. 대부분의 교실 수업의 상호작용은 Initiation-Response-Feedback(IRF), 즉 교사가 질문하고 학생들이 대답한 뒤 학생들의 대답에 대한 피드백의 형태를 띤다.

> * The teacher *initiates* an assertion or asks a question.
> * The students *responds*.
> * The teacher *provides feedback* in order to encourage students to think and to perform at higher levels (e.g. "Tell me more! Are you saying that...?)

본 담화 형태에서 교사는 assisting questions로 학습자가 내용과 주제에 초점을 둬 생각하고 자신의 생각을 보다 정교하게 말할 수 있도록 유도한다. 가령, 교사는 "What do you mean by that?" / "That's incredible" / "Could you explain that a little more?" 등의 assisting question을 제시할 수 있다. 누가 말을 하고 언제 해야 할 것인지를 교사에 의해 통제받는 IRE의 담화 구조에서 지배적인 교실 수업을 받고 있는 학습자들은 자연스럽게 대화에 참여하며 자연스러운 turn-taking을 할 수 있는 기회를 제공받아야 한다.

2 Teaching Pronunciation

발음 지도는 발음의 두 가지 요소인 segmentals와 suprasegmentals에 대한 지도가 모두 명시적이고 유의미하게 진행돼야 한다. 이 두 요소 모두 실제 학습자의 목표 언어 사용에서의 이해 가능한 발음(intelligibility)에 영향을 끼치기 때문이다.

(1) Bottom-up Approach

언어의 분절적인 요소, 즉 음소의 정확한 발음에 초점을 두는 접근법은 모국어의 간섭 현상을 많이 받기 때문에 대조분석을 토대로 발음 지도를 하되, 유의미한 의사소통 안에서 개별 음가의 최소대립쌍을 제공하는 것이 좋다(contextualized minimal pairs).

Bottom-up approach focuses on segmentals, clear articulation, practising *minimal pairs*. Segmentals consist of the phonemes of the language, or its smallest meaningful units. In the past pronunciation instruction usually focused on the articulation of consonants and vowels and the discrimination of minimal pairs. The teacher's job is to identify those areas that affect intelligibility the most and to find ways to integrate practice of those pronunciation features into the lesson.

Example

Meaningful Minimal Pairs

Student A's Worksheet

Directions: Read sentences 1-4 to your partner, and then circle the words you hear in sentences 5-8 as they are read by your partner.

1. He gave me a hug.
2. Hand me the pin.
3. This room is full of cats.
4. The men will come soon.
5. I'd like to see the chimp / champ.
6. That's my luck / lock.
7. They spun / spin around.
8. I fell over a rock / rack.

Student B's Worksheet

Directions: Circle the words in sentences 1-4 as they are read by your partner, and then read sentences 5-8 to your partner.

1. He gave me a hug / hog.
2. Hand me the pen / pin.
3. This room is full of cots / cats.
4. The man / men will come soon.
5. I'd like to see the champ.
6. That's my lock.
7. They spun around.
8. I fell over a rock.

Plus ➕

UNIT 1. −ed endings

A. Listen to the example. Listen again and repeat the utterance.

walked /t/ dreamed /d/ started /ed/

B. Do you hear /t/, /d/, or /ed/? Listen and check [✓].

	/t/	/d/	/ed/
1. listened			
2. stopped			
3. watched			
4. needed			
5. played			
6. checked			
7. exercised			
8. wanted			

C. Practice the conversations below with a partner.

1. A: Did you drive here?

   B: No, I walked.

2. A: What time did you start?

   B: I started at about 3:00.

3. A: What did you do last night?

   B: Oh, I just listened to music.

4. A: Why did you go to the store?

   B: I needed some bread.

5. A: What did you do last night?

   B: Nothing special. I watched a boring movie on TV.

6. A: Did you have fun yesterday?

   B: Yes! I played baseball with my friends.

(Practical English Language Teaching Speaking)

Comments:

It is often the case that pronunciation issues interact with grammar issues. As a result, if learners mispronounce key sounds, it can seem like they are producing ungrammatical utterances. One very important grammar point that beginning learners often work on is the past tense and other cases were verbs end in *−ed*. Depending on the surrounding sounds, the *−ed ending* can be pronounced in three different ways. Also, particularly for beginning learners in EFL situations, and especially for those who have had mostly reading exposure to English (not much listening exposure), there is sometimes a tendency to pronounce the *−ed* as if it were a syllable no matter where it occurs. For instance, students may correctly say "hunted" as two syllables, but then also say "roped" as "ro−ped" or "pulled" as "pull−ed" because the spelling suggests that *−ed* is a syllable to be said. For learners whose native language doesn't use consonant clusters at the end of words, pronouncing the English past tense and other *−ed* endings can be very difficult. It will take some practice on learners' part and some explanation on yours.

(2) Top-down Approach

억양, 강세 및 리듬의 초분절적인 요소는 의미에 직접적인 영향을 끼치므로 적절한 지도가 이뤄지지 않을 경우 의사소통에 장애가 될 뿐 아니라 때로는 무례한 듯한 인상을 남길 수 있다.

Top-down approach focuses on <u>suprasegmentals</u> (intonation, rhythm, stress). Suprasegmentals include intonation, rhythm, and stress. These features can have an even greater impact on <u>intelligibility</u> than the mispronunciation of sounds. Thus, the focus has shifted to fluency rather than accuracy encouraging an emphasis on suprasegmentals.

Word stress	• Now, you need to add cóld cream. • Now, you need to add cold créam.
Sentence stress	• I lost my **red** scarf. (not the blue one) • I lost my red **scarf**. (not my red hat)
Intonation	• She's my sister, Marcia(↘) (Marcia is your sister) • She's my sister, Marcia(↗) (You're identifying your sister for someone else named Marcia)
Word group & pause	• Would you like the Super Salad? • Would you like the soup⁀or salad?

(3) Balanced View

최근의 발음 지도는 원어민과 같은 정확한 발음이나 강세가 아닌 이해 가능한 발음(intelligibility)에 초점을 두고 있으며, 이해 가능한 발음에 영향을 끼치는 분절적인 요소와 초분절적인 요소를 의사소통의 맥락 내에서 조화를 이루도록 가르치고 있다.

Balanced view focuses on <u>intelligibility</u> (bottom-up & top-down). In recent years, emphasis on meaning and communicative intent alone will not suffice to achieve grammatical accuracy and teaching pronunciation has emerged from the segmental/suprasegmental debate to a more balanced view, which recognizes that a lack of intelligibility can be attributed to both micro and macro features.

3 Error Treatment

유창성을 넘어서 정확성에도 목적을 둔 교사는 학생이 생성한 오류의 수정 유무를 판단하고, 수정을 할 경우 언제·어떤 방식으로 피드백을 제공할 것인지 결정하고 적절한 피드백을 선택한 뒤 제공해야 한다.

> - Should learners' errors be corrected?
> - When should learners' errors be corrected?
> - How should errors be corrected?
> - Who should do the correcting?

(1) To What and When? – 어떤 오류를 언제 수정할 것인가?

교사는 학습자들의 참여를 유도하기 위해서 학생의 오류를 하나의 학습 과정으로 인식하고, 오류 수정은 학습 목표에 따라 진행해야 한다. 즉, 교실 수업의 목표가 정확성에 있는 경우 즉각적으로 피드백을 제공하지만 의사소통에 초점을 둘 경우 의사소통 활동이 끝난 후에 피드백을 제공하는 것이 바람직하다.

When the focus is on meaning, it is inappropriate to interrupt the flow of interaction. In these situations, the teacher can make a note of errors for follow-up treatment later. When the focus is on form, the teacher might well interrupt before the students have finished their turn.

(2) How? – 어떤 피드백을 제공할 것인가?

① Indirect/Implicit feedback: 묵시적으로 교사가 오류를 수정하거나 오류가 있음을 암시하는 전략으로, 정확성보다는 의미에 초점을 두는 경우 사용한다. 묵시적 전략은 학습자의 자가 수정(self-correction)을 유도할 수 있지만 학습자가 오류를 알아차리지 못할 수도 있다.

ⓐ **Recast**: A teacher reformulates all parts of a student's utterance minus the error.

> Ex T: What did you do this weekend?
> S: I have gone to the movies.
> T: Oh, *you went to the movies last night*. What did you see?

ⓑ **Clarification request**: A teacher uses phrases such as "Pardon me?" or "I don't understand." or asks another questions such as "What do you mean by that?". This request signals to the students that there was some kind of error, or something was not clear in their language use, and invites them to reformulate their utterance. Teachers use this feedback when students make meaning related errors while the focus is on communication.

> Ex　T: How old are you?
> 　　　S: Thirty.
> 　　　T: *Pardon me?*
> 　　　S: Thirteen.

② **Direct/Explicit feedback**: 명시적으로 학습자의 오류를 지적하는 전략으로, 교사가 정확한 답을 제공하거나 혹은 오류가 있는 부분을 지적함으로써 학습자가 자신의 오류에 대해 주목을 하게 된다. 보다 효과적인 언어 습득을 위해서는 교사가 정답을 제공하기보다는 학습자 스스로 수정하도록 유도하는 것이 바람직하다.

ⓐ **Explicit correction**: The teacher directly tells a student what a mistake was and provides the correct answer. For example, she might say, "oh, you mcan...," or "you should say...," or "the correct form of this verb form is..." An alternative of this strategy is to ask a peer student, other than the one who committed the error, to provide the correct answer.

> Ex　T: Where did you go after class yesterday?
> 　　　S: I go home.
> 　　　T: 'Go' is not the correct past tense form. *You need to say, "I went home."*

③ **Guided feedback**: A more effective strategy than direct correction is to provide the students an opportunity to self-repair and guide them toward the correct answer. Strategies that allow the teacher to do so are normally referred to as elicitation techniques. The purpose of such strategies is to help the students notice that something was wrong, locate the mistake(s), and/or provide metalinguistic feedback, that is, some information about the mistakes.

ⓐ **Metalinguistic feedback**: It contains either <u>comments, information</u> regarding the accuracy of a student's utterance without providing the correct form.

- **Providing general reminders**: The teacher can also provide general reminders simply by referring to a particular lesson or class. In doing so, the teacher activates grammatical rules the student has dealt with before.

  > **Ex** T: Where did you go after class yesterday?
  > S: I go home.
  > T: *Do you remember the grammar we focused on in class yesterday?*

- **Asking questions**: The teacher asks a particular question about the mistake. For example, "How do we say this in English?" By asking specific questions, most teachers indirectly provide some information about what a student's actual mistake was. This strategy is also a form of metalinguistic feedback.

  > **Ex** T: Where are you going later?
  > S: I am going later shopping on.
  > T: *What should be the correct word order in your sentence?*

ⓑ **Repetition (pinpointing)**: There are different ways of <u>pointing out which part of a student's utterance is wrong and in need of repair.</u> One strategy is <u>to echo the faulty utterance.</u> The teacher repeats the students' ill-formed utterance without correction, but pronounces the feature with exaggeration.

> **Ex** S: On the table there's a red cup.
> T: Um, hmm, but you said "*a Red Cup*" (Emphasizing) What else?

ⓒ **Elicitation (pausing)**: Another strategy involves pausing. The instructor <u>repeats the learner's utterance up to the point of the error,</u> where the student needs to self-correct.

> **Ex** T: Where are you going later?
> S: I am go to the supermarket?
> T: *I am...*
> S: I am going to the supermarket.

(3) Uptake

Uptake is defined in their work as "a student's utterance that immediately follows the teachers' feedback and that constitutes a reaction in some way to the teachers' intention to draw attention to some aspect of the initial utterance." Put another way, uptake shows what the student tries to do with the teacher's feedback.

Two types of student uptake appear: uptake that produces an utterances still needing repair and uptake that produces a repair of the error on which the teacher's feedback focused. The latter type—uptake with repair—does not include self-initiated repair but rather those types of repairs that students produced in direct response: to the feedback provided by the teacher.

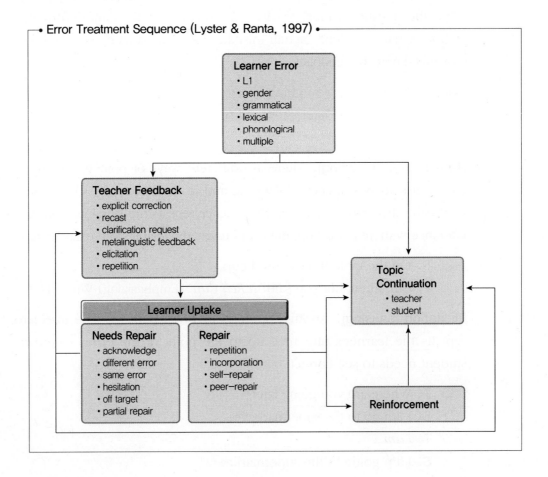

• Error Treatment Sequence (Lyster & Ranta, 1997) •

02 \ Teaching Writing

1 Product vs. Process−oriented Approach

(1) Product-oriented Approach & Process-oriented Approach

Product−oriented approach는 글쓰기 활동(writing)의 과정보다 그 결과물(product, outcome)에 초점을 두고 오류가 없는 완벽한 쓰기 활동을 지향하는 반면, process−oriented approach는 글쓰기 활동을 하니의 사고 과정이라 생각하고 작가의 생각을 글로 옮기는 과정을 중시하는 접근법이다. 따라서 무엇을 쓰느냐가 아니라 어떻게 쓰느냐에 초점을 두고 글을 수정하는 과정 자체를 중시한다.

Whereas the product approach focuses on writing tasks in which the learner imitates, copies and transforms models provided by the teacher and/or the textbook, the process approach focuses on the steps involved in creating a piece of work. The primary goal of product writing is an error-free coherent text. Process writing allows for the fact that no text can be perfect, but that a writer will get closer to perfection by producing, reflecting on, discussing, and reworking successive draft of text.

Product-oriented Approach	Process-oriented Approach
• internal revision (revising in order to clarify meaning for oneself) • writer-based prose • quality	• external revision (revising in order to clarify meaning for the reader) • reader-based prose • quantity

Example 1

Product-oriented Approach

Teaching Procedure: Dicto-comp

1. The teacher shows pictures of pets to students and asks what kinds of pets they like.
2. The teacher gives each of the students a short story of a dog and a set of four sequential pictures showing its storyline, telling them that they are going to read and write the story as accurately as possible. The story contains a number of regular past tense verbs.
3. Students read the story silently for 3 minutes and return the story to the teacher but keep the pictures.
4. After putting some key words from the story on the board, the teacher reads the whole story aloud.
5. With the aid of the pictures and key words, students write the story as closely as they can remember.
6. The teacher collects students' writings and later corrects them by crossing out incorrect regular past tense forms, providing corresponding correct forms above them.
7. In the next class, students receive their writings and look over their errors and the teacher's corrections.

Example 2

Process-oriented Approach

Teaching Procedure: Essay writing

1. The teacher sets up guidelines on how to write essays.
2. The teacher explains to the students how to use multimedia during the writing process.
3. The teacher collects the first drafts of the students' essays via e-mail.
4. The teacher opens up an online blog for the class to post the first drafts of their essays.
5. Each student reads one of his/her peers' essays and posts three well-thought-out feedback statements on the blog.
6. The teacher asks the students to read the feedback received from their peers and to revise their first drafts. When they have questions about the feedback, they should e-mail them to their feedback providers.
7. The teacher gives his/her own feedback to each student via e-mail.
8. The teacher asks the students to post their revised essays on the blog.

(2) Writing Approach for the Lower Level Students

영어 수준이 낮은 학생들에게 쓰기 지도를 하기 위해서 process-oriented approach와 product-oriented approach를 혼합해 사용할 수 있다. 즉, 학생들의 글쓰기 과정을 통제해 topic에 대한 정보를 효과적으로 구성하고 어떻게 text화를 할지 가르치거나, 또는 실제적인 글쓰기를 진행하면서 자신의 글에 대해 수정할 기회를 제공하는 것이다. 가령, 과정 중심 글쓰기 안에서 산출 중심의 글쓰기가 일부 사용되는 수업 전개를 토대로 lower level 학생들의 글쓰기에 대한 두려움, 또는 쓰기 과업에 대한 부담감(cognitive load)을 낮출 수 있을 것이다.

(3) Teaching Procedure

① The teacher divides students into groups and asks them to work cooperatively and write down all the ideas that come to mind in connection with the given topic.

교사는 주어진 topic에 대한 group brainstorming을 진행하면서 학생들이 보다 적극적이고 자유롭게 자신의 생각을 이끌어 낼 수 있도록 학생들이 필요로 하는 language support 외에 뒤로 물러나 학생들의 참여를 독려해야 한다. 또한, 교사는 학생들의 idea에 대한 평가를 하지 않아야 한다.

② The teacher encourages students to extend their ideas into a mind map, spidergram or linear form.

이 단계에서 학생들은 자신의 생각에 대한 평가를 할 수 있다. 가령, 주제와 관련해 자신의 idea에 대한 quality와 usefulness에 대한 판단을 하게 된다. 요컨대, Mind-map이나 spidergram은 학생들의 주제와 관련된 정보들을 조직해서 보여줌으로써 손쉽게 글쓰기로 연결되며, 글의 구조 등을 잡는 데 도움이 된다.

③ The teacher provides a model text and students read it by focusing on coherence and cohesion of a model text.

▶ **Coherence** refers to the logical development of ideas within a text and it is an important subskill for students to be aware of.

▶ **Cohesion** refers to the grammatical and lexical connections between individual clauses. The grammatical links can be classified such as referents (pronouns, the article "the", demonstrative), ellipsis (leaving out of a words or phrases where they are unnecessary), and conjunction (a word joins phrases or clauses together).

교사는 text의 coherence와 cohesion을 위해 다음과 같은 다양한 활동을 진행할 수 있다.

ⓐ Focusing on the topic and function of each paragraph

ⓑ Examining how the writer has chosen to order his arguments

ⓒ Showing how to make their text "reader friendly"

ⓓ Asking students to circle all the pronouns and then to use arrows to connect them to their referent

ⓔ Asking students to replace a sentence which is missing from each paragraph or to replace the first sentence of each paragraph

ⓕ Matching clauses which have been separated

ⓖ Gapping conjunctions which students must replace from a selection.

④ The teacher asks students to write the first draft of their texts with a partner.

교사는 본격적인 글쓰기 활동을 pair work으로 진행하면서 실제 글쓰기는 reader와 writer 간의 실질적이고 협력적(cooperative)인 과업이라는 것을 학생으로 하여금 깨닫게 할 수 있다. 개별적 글쓰기는 writer가 reader에게 가지는 막연한 생각을 토대로 일어나지만, pair work으로 진행되는 cooperative writing은 학생들이 각각 writer이면서 동시에 reader가 될 수 있으므로 실질적(realistic)이고 상호작용적(interactive)인 글쓰기 과업이 될 수 있다.

> ▶ Fast and collaborative writing
>
> The students write quickly on a topic for five to ten minutes without worrying about correct language or punctuation. Writing as quickly as possible, if they can't think of a word, they leave a space or write it in their own language. The important thing is to keep writing. At the same time collaborative writing can be quite motivating. It enables the stronger students to help the weaker ones.
>
> ▶ Whole class text construction, composing on the blackboard and parallel writing
> These techniques have their foundation in product writing but are effective in providing a framework for lower level students to work from. These techniques can develop a sense of collective achievement, while eliminating fear of being left to "go it alone", completely unguided.

⑤ When students consult each other and co-construct texts, the teacher moves around listening to their comments, providing feedback or answering questions on structure, lexical items, the validity of an argument, the order of presentation of the information, etc.

학생들의 과업 수행 시 교사는 필요한 도움 및 정보를 제공해 줄 수 있으며, 학생들의 과업 효율성 및 빈번한 질문 등을 메모하고, 오류 분석 활동을 위해 부정확하게 사용된 표현 등을 기록하도록 한다.

⑥ The teacher asks students to edit their text (self-editing/peer editing).

이 단계에서 교사는 학생들에게 자신이 쓴 글에서 사용한 목표 언어에 대한 평가를 하도록 하고, 자신이 범한 오류를 찾아가면서 text를 점검해 수정·보완하고 개선하도록 할 수 있다. 또한, reader 입장에서 동료들의 text를 읽고 수정해야 할 부분 (better organization, paragraph divisions, sentence variety, vocabulary choice)을 명확히 제시할 수 있으며, 반복적인 어휘 사용이나 문법적인 오류 및 잘못된 철자 등을 지적해 서로의 editor 역할을 수행하도록 한다. 이때, 교사는 필요하면 written feedback을 제공하도록 할 수도 있다.

⑦ The teacher asks students to write the second draft based on self- and peer editing. Then, he or she responds to students' second drafts suitably.

교사는 학생들의 글에 대한 평가를 할 때, 우선적으로 positive comments를 제공해 학생들의 글쓰기에 대한 자신감을 심어줄 수 있으며, 다음 번 글쓰기 수업에 대한 기대감을 키울 수 있다. 유용한 평가가 되기 위해 교사는 학생들이 필요로 하는 것에 기반을 두도록 한다.

> ▶ When students still favor comments on the grammatical and lexical correctness of their work, the teacher can use an *error correction code*, which serves to highlight the error but still requires the students to reflect on what the error actually is.

⑧ The teacher returns the drafts and then students write the final draft based upon teacher feedback.

Plus ⊕

Some Classroom Techniques Based on Process-oriented Approach

1. Pre-writing Stage

① **목적**: 다양한 아이디어를 찾는 단계로, 글의 정확성보다는 내용의 다양성이나 참신함 등에 초점을 둔다.

② **활동**

ⓐ Brainstorming
- It is often a group exercise in which all students in the class are encouraged to participate by sharing their collective knowledge about a particular subject.
- A teacher suggests a broad topic.
- Students call out as many associations as possible.
- The teacher can then write on the board.

ⓑ Freewriting (quickwriting)
- The main idea of this technique is for students to write for a specific period time (usually 5-10 minutes) without stopping.
- Free from the necessity of worrying about grammar and format.
- A teacher provides an opening clause or sentence for the students to start with.
- After copying this sentence, students write down whatever comes into their heads.
- The freewriting generated can be raw material to use in addressing the writing assignment at hand.

ⓒ Clustering (wordmapping)
- Clustering begins with a key word or central idea placed in the center of a page around which the student jots down in a few minutes all of the free associations triggered by the subject matter.
- The words or phrases generated are put on the page or board in a pattern which takes shapes from the connections the writer sees as each new thought emerges.
- Writers can be exposed to a wide variety of approaches to the topic which might further generate material for writing.
- It can get in touch with the right-hemisphere part of the brain.

2. While—and Post Writing Stage

① **목적**: 본격적인 작문과 점검 활동이 일어난다. 점검 활동은 먼저 내용의 적합성(appropriateness)에서 시작해 글의 정확성(accuracy)으로 초점이 이동한다.

② **활동**

ⓐ **Peer—editing (after first draft)**: Students step out of their own selves, to see what they have created through the eyes of others to discover the impact of their words on the thoughts of their readers, so that they can then use the information to improve what we have written. We call this peer—editing. Not only does each student get feedback from his or her classmates but he or she also gives feedback to them.

> Ex A checklist can be very short and used first by the students to check a writing and then by the teacher to evaluate it focusing attention on the critical features of one particular task:
> - Which sentence expresses the main idea?
> - Which sentence develops that main idea?
> - Is every verb in the correct tense?
> - Have you used the correct form of each tense?

쓰기 활동에서 초점을 둔 항목(예: main idea의 표현이나 올바른 동사 시제의 사용 여부 등)에 점수를 부여함으로써 학생들이 활동의 목적을 얼마나 달성했는지, 얼마나 발전했는지를 확인할 수 있다. 또한, checklist에 쓰기 수업 중 다룬 중요한 요소를 포함하고 학습의 효과를 극대화해 쓰기 능력을 키워 나갈 수 있다.

ⓑ **Proofreading (after second draft)**: After you (the student) have rewritten your paper, go over it carefully to see if the language sounds are correct and if your message seems complete and understandable. Finally, submit your paper to your teacher.

ⓒ **Conferencing (using teacher's feedback)**: As the class writes, the teacher can talk with individual students about work in progress. Through careful questioning, the teacher can support a student writer in getting ideas together, organizing them, and finding appropriate language. Also, in a one—to—one conference, the teacher can ask the student to read a section aloud. Frequently the students will then spot errors like an unfinished sentence, a confused sentence, or an omitted word. Some teachers, during a discussion about a topic with a student, make notes of what the student says. The teacher's written notes then form the basis for further prewriting activities.

명료하게 표현하지 않은 학습자가 의도한 의미를 이끌어 내기 위해 교사는 학습자의 글에 대한 토론(conferencing)을 시도할 수 있다. 이때, 학습자는 conferencing을 통해 자신의 오류를 고치거나 불완전한 문장을 보다 명료하고 완전하게 고칠 수 있으며, 교사는 이를 다음 작문활동의 pre−단계에서 활용할 수 있다.

Ex T: Your first sentence tells the reader one of the reasons why you like puppies. It is a good beginning. Why else do you like puppies?

S: Well. Um. They're cute.

T: Do you know any puppies?

S: Yeah.

T: Can you tell me anything else about the puppy that you know?

S: Well. Um. My puppy is happy when I come home.

T: What is your puppy's name?

S: Argos.

T: You have a really good beginning. Why don't you write about Argos and how Argos feels when you come home?

S: OK.

2 How to Respond to Students Writing

학생들의 글을 평가하거나 피드백을 제공할 경우 전체적인 평가나 점수를 매기기 전 학생들의 글을 한 번 훑어봄으로써 글의 전반적인 목적 및 주장을 파악해 볼 필요가 있다.

(1) When you pick up a student's writing, don't immediately reach for a pen or pencil. Read the whole piece through first before you write anything. That is, you may want to skim through four or five papers to get a sense of the pile before reading and grading any single paper. Many teachers read each paper once through to grasp the overall argument before making any marks. Whether skimming on a first time through or reading carefully, you might keep the fixed categories in mind, which will help you assess the paper's strengths and weaknesses:

Ex *When I was faced with up to 40 students' written products to respond to in just a week, I realized that the standards I applied to the first few were different from those I applied to the last few. I might have been much stricter or easy-going on those first few written products.*

① Thesis

- Is there one main argument in the paper?
- Does it fulfill the assignment?
- Is the thesis clearly stated near the beginning of the paper?
- Is it interesting, complex?
- Is it argued throughout?

② Structure

- Is the paper clearly organized?
- Is it easy to understand the main point of each paragraph?
- Does the order of the overall argument make sense, and is it easy to follow?

③ Evidence and Analysis

Does the paper offer supporting evidence for each of its points?

④ Style

- Is the style appropriate for its audience?
- Is the paper concise and to the point?
- Are sentences clear and grammatically correct?
- Are there spelling or proofreading errors?

(2) Look for strengths as well as weaknesses, and let the student know what the strengths are. All students as good writers, need to know what they're doing well so that they can do it again in the future. Remember to give specific examples.

> Ex *Your first sentence tells the reader one of the reasons why we should save the earth. It is a good beginning! / It is easy to understand the main point of each paragraph and it is easy to follow.*

On the other hand, you should discuss the paper's weaknesses, focusing on large problems first. You don't have to comment on every little thing that went wrong in a paper. Instead, choose two or three of the most important areas in which the student needs to improve, and present these in order of descending importance. You may find it useful to key these weaknesses to such essay elements as Thesis, Structure, Evidence, and Style. *Give specific examples* to show the student what you're seeing. If possible, suggest practical solutions so that the student writer can correct the problems in the next paper.

Example ❶

My family is a large family, having six people (live) together in the house. Each one has different way to help (them) relax. And also the way they thought is relaxing, having give me too much angry. ⟩ ?

For example, my youngest sister (is love) chinese music, (therefor) whenever (she at home do her) home-work, always has the music on. That bother me a lot. Because she and I live in the same room (making) me

have to stop with the (arcurment) with her. ?

But the most angry is get up in the morning with ? a disco music. That (rely) make me crazy. That whole day I just have bad feeling. That is my youngest brother (relax's) way. *to relax*

Written Feedback on Student Weakness of the above written product:

You have told us about two members of your family. Now I am wondering what the others do to relax! Do they like music too? Read this aloud. If any sentences seem unclear, try writing them again. See if you can express the ideas in sentences 3, 4, and 8 more simply. Check the spelling of the three words I have underlined.

학생들의 writing에 대한 comment는 paraphrase of the ideas, praise, questions, or suggestions 등의 형식을 띠는데, 물론 'good' or 'need more work' 등을 첨언할 수 있다. 무엇보다 중요한 것은 학생들이 comment를 통해 자신의 writing을 보다 나은 글로 고치기 위한 무언가를 얻을 수 있어야 한다는 것이다. 특히, first draft일 경우 grammar나 spelling mistakes보다는 ideas나 organization에 대한 comments를 제공하는 것이 바람직하다.

Example ❷

> Ever since I was a small child the magic of tricks always were mysterious to me. One person who I believed was a master of it is Harry Houdini. He was the greatest and his magic will live on as the greatest. If I was to meet him at my magic dinner, all my mysteries would be answer. May he will even teach me a trick to amaze my friends. I feel I'm the person who should find out the secrets that were buried with him.
>
> **Written Comments on Student Weakness of the above written product:**
> *You have made me very interested in Houdini. What did he do that was so great? What mysteries do you want to be answered? What exactly were the secrets that were buried with him? I'd like to know.*

두 번째 학생 글에 대한 교사의 피드백은 'questions'을 토대로 글에 대한 불명확한 content organization과 세부 정보에 대한 부족(lack of details)을 글의 단점으로 지적해 주고 있고, 질문을 통해 어떤 정보가 보충돼야 할지 방향을 제시해 주고 있다.

(3) Work out your own strategy for handling errors and explain it to your students. If you use any editing symbols, make sure that the students are familiar with all of them and know what to do when they see one.

Example ❶

Correction Symbols (Error Correction Code)

Symbol	Meaning	Example error
S	A spelling error	The asnwer is obvious.
WO	A mistake in word order	I like very much it.
G	A grammar mistake	I am going to buy some furnitures.
T	Wrong verb tense	I have seen him yesterday.
C	Concord mistake Ex the subject and verb agreement	People is angry.
∧	Something has been left out.	He told ∧ that he was sorry.
WW	Wrong word	I am interested on jazz music.
{ }	Something is not necessary.	He was not {too} strong enough.
?M	The meaning is unclear.	That is a very excited photograph.
P	A punctuation mistake	Do you like london?
F/I	Too formal or informal	Hi Mr. Franklin, Thank you for your letter...

Decide if you will correct or simply *indicate* where they occur, if you will deal only with the errors you have discussed in class, with errors of a certain type, or with all errors; decide what importance you attach to grammatical errors and, again, let your students know. Provide opportunities for the students to use the symbols, too.

다만, 교사가 학생들의 작문에서 발견되는 모든 오류들을 수정해 줄 수는 없기 때문에 수업 시간에 다룬 문법 요소(learning points)나 의미 전달에 방해가 되는 오류(global error)에 초점을 둔다. 또한, 학생들이 범한 빈번한 오류에 대한 면밀한 규명이 필요하며, 다음 수업 활동에 이를 반영한 수업 계획(plan our lesson)을 세운다.

Example ❷

Correction Codes

> Harry Greenman
>
> The spaceship landed. A door opened. Harry the Greenman
> V   stumbled and fell out of the spaceship. He mumble something
> ww sp that anybody could understand but than a bit louder. My name
>   ^   is captain Greenman and I want study your language. "Who
>   is Director of this school?"
>   Frank, a tall man gave to understand that he is the boss and they
>   sp arranged some lessons. Next morning Frank thought some
> ww V grammar. But the lesson was very bored. Captain Greenman felt
>   asleep. Frank was very angry and threw the greenman back in
> wo the spaceship. Suddenly came another creature out. It was Mrs
>   Greenman. She hit the director and turned back into the
>   spaceship.

(Jim Scrivener, Learning Teaching)

Codes can *indicate* where an error is and what type of error it is. However, they leave the learners to do some work in order to *find the corrections for themselves.*

이러한 error correction code를 사용하는 경우 학생들에게 자신이 어디에 오류를 범했고, 어떻게 수정해야 할지에 대한 정보를 제공해 스스로 오류에 대한 수정(self-correction)을 이끌어 낼 수 있기 때문에 lexical & grammatical error에 대한 세심한 집중을 유도할 수 있다. 그러나 error correction code를 통해서 지적할 수 있는 오류들은 한정적이며, 지나친 지적은 학생들을 의기소침하게 만들 수 있다 (Filter is up). 따라서, 교사는 학생들이 반드시 알아야 할 오류 순으로 지적을 해 학생들의 집중을 유도하는 것이 보다 효과적일 것이다.

It often seems inappropriate to point out every error; it can be dispiriting to get back work with a large quantity of marks on it. The teacher probably needs to decide which errors she thinks most important or useful for the student to work on at the moment and then to draw attention to these.

In a conclusion, remember that when you or any other reader responds to a student's piece of writing, your main job is not to pass judgement on its quality, but to help the writer see what to do next. Ask yourself: what should the writer do now to improve this paper?

3 Controlled to Free Writing Techniques

(1) Controlled (Intensive) Writing

교실 수업에서 진행되는 문법에 초점을 둔 쓰기 활동과 평가를 위한 통제형 연습 문제가 해당된다.

Controlled writing can fit into a composition curriculum at any level of student ability in these two places. Before free writing use the text as a source of vocabulary, ideas, idioms, and organization to help them in planning their own piece of writing. After free writing see what problems your students are having and assign a controlled task to give them practice with the problem area.

① **Controlled composition**: 특정 문법 항목과 어휘 등에 초점을 둔 연습 활동을 말한다.

ⓐ Controlled composition focuses the students' attention on specific features of the written language.

ⓑ It is a good method of reinforcing grammar, vocabulary, and syntax in context.

ⓒ Students can be aware of the conventions of written English such as indentation, punctuation, connecting words, and spelling.

Example ❶

Students work in small groups to agree on each change in this passage:

You are a police detective who has been following a man every day for a month. You write this report for your supervisor;

"Every day, C.P. gets up at 7 a.m. He walks to a local store to buy a newspaper. He reads the obituaries. Then he makes three different telephone calls from three different public pay phones. He goes to a coffee shop and waits outside. A tall blond woman driving a silver Cadillac picks him up."

Your supervisor then tells you that she wants a specific report on what C.P. did on Wednesday last week. Change the report. Begin with "Last Wednesday, C.P. got up at 7 a.m."

② **Sentence combining**: 둘 이상의 짧은 문장을 하나로 합치는 연습 활동을 통해서 문장의 다양성과 문장 구조를 익힐 수 있다.

Sentence combining exercises improve students' sentence structure, length of sentence, and sentence variety.

Example ❷

Combine the following sentences to one sentence.

1. a. He visits his grandmother every weekend.
   b. His grandmother lives in Westwood.
   ➡ He visits his grandmother in Westwood every weekend.

2. a. It is early morning.
   b. Gus is driving to work.
   ➡ _____

3. a. He sees a hitchhiker.
   b. The hitchhiker is by the road.
   c. He stops his car.
   d. He stops to give the hitchhiker a ride.
   ➡ _____

③ **Dicto-composition**: Dictogloss와 같은 방식으로 진행된다. 즉 교사가 텍스트를 2~3번 들려주면 학생들이 텍스트를 재구성하는데, dictogloss는 듣기에 초점을 둔 반면 dicto-comp는 쓰기에 초점을 둔 활동이다.

A paragraph is read at normal speed, usually two or three times. Then the teacher asks students to rewrite the paragraph to the best of their recollection of the reading. In one of several variations of the dicto-comp technique, the teacher, after reading the passage, puts key words from the paragraph, in sequence, on the chalkboard as cues for the students.

Example ❸

This is a procedure for teaching writing designed by a middle school English teacher.

1. The teacher shows pictures of pets to students and asks what kinds of pets they like.

2. The teacher gives each of the students a short story of a dog and a set of four sequential pictures showing its storyline, telling them that they are going to read and write the story as accurately as possible. The story contains a number of regular past tense verbs.

3. Students read the story silently for 3 minutes and return the story to the teacher but keep the pictures.

4. After putting some key words from the story on the board, the teacher reads the whole story aloud.

5. With the aid of the pictures and key words, students write the story as closely as they can remember.

6. The teacher collects students' writings and later corrects them by crossing out incorrect regular past tense forms, providing corresponding correct forms above them.

7. In the next class, students receive their writings and look over their errors and the teacher's corrections.

Plus ➕

Guided Writing

내용 혹은 문법에 초점을 둔 활동으로, 특정 구문 혹은 특정 내용을 제시하고 학생이 이를 바탕으로 쓰기 활동을 하게 된다.

Guided writing is an extension of controlled writing. It is less controlled than the controlled writing in that it gives students some but not all of the content and form of the sentences they will use. Their finished products will be similar but no exactly alike. Students are given a first or last sentence, an outline to fill out, a series of questions to respond to or information to include in their piece of writing.

1. Question and Answer

학습자의 쓰기 활동을 위해 문장의 구조를 질문의 형식으로 제시한다. 논리적으로 구성된 질문들은 그 답변들을 배열했을 때 하나의 텍스트를 이룰 수도 있다.

The type of controlled composition that uses question and answer format allows students a little more freedom in structuring sentences. They are not given the actual text that they will write; rather, they are given a series of questions, the answers to which form the text. Carefully constructed questions will produce a coherent text.

2. Example 1

Questions can ask about information which is given in notes or a list or even in a picture sequence. The following list shows an army recruit's daily routine:

6:00 get up	6:25 march to the mess hall
6:05 make bed	6:30 eat breakfast
6:10 polish boots and buttons	6:45 do exercises
6:20 put on uniform	

The students write a paragraph that describes the daily routine of Billy, a new recruit, by answering the following questions in complete sentences. If students are able to, they could also combine some of the sentences.

- When does Billy get up?
- What does he do first?
- What does he do next?
- What does he do then?
- When does he march to the mess hall?
- What does he do there?
- What does he do after breakfast?
- Is the beginning of this day leisurely or very busy?

3. Example 2

Students look at and discuss the picture and any new vocabulary words or idioms are written on the board. Then they are given these guidelines for writing.

Step 1. Write three paragraphs about Grant Wood's painting American Gothic.

a. Begin by telling your reader that the picture shows a couple standing in front of a house. Then describe the house: tell your reader if it is in the city or the country, what it is made of, and what color it is. If it reminds you of any other type of building, mention that also.

b. Start your second paragraph by saying something about the woman: Is she, for example, young, old, pretty, stern-looking, simply dressed? Then write a sentence each about her hair, her facial expression, and her clothes.

c. Begin your last paragraph with "Standing next to the woman is a man." Go on to tell your reader if you think he is her husband, and why or why not. Then write a sentence each about his features, his glasses, his expression, his clothes, and the tool he is holding.

Step 2. Now discuss with your classmates and your teacher what two or three sentences you could write to finish off the piece of writing.

(2) Free Writing

학습자들의 생각이나 실제 생활(real life)과 관련지어 자유로운 쓰기 활동을 한다.

> ▶ Dialogue journals: 학생이 수업 내용이나 수업에서의 느낌 등을 작성하면 이를 교사가 읽고 교사의 생각을 쓰는 일종의 교사와 학생 간의 대화 노트로, 이때 교사는 학생의 dialogue journal에 대해서 평가 혹은 비평을 해서는 안 된다.

Dialogue journals enable students and teachers to interact on a one-toone basis at any level and in any learning context. They are very useful communicative events at the early stages of learning to write in a new language.

① Topics in dialogue journals are typically not assigned, so that the partners are free to discuss whatever they wish.

② They enable the beginner to generate some personal input and receive the teacher's direct feedback on it.

③ They can be done via e-mail and the communication between students and teachers can take on this more modern form of interaction.

④ The writing is not corrected, graded or evaluated.

⑤ Teachers need to keep the writing private, promising not to show the journal to a third party.

⑥ The focus on communication provides a non-threatening, high-interest interchange that features a sense of equality between and renders the relationship between teacher and learner less hierarchical.

⑦ The process emphasizes meaning rather than form; the language input that the learner receives from the teacher is comprehensible; correct grammatical forms are modeled by the teacher, thus taught indirectly.

Example

Name Elizabeth
Date 05-14-02

Journal Topic Countries

What i like about my country. The Food.
weather. Sontime Friend Family sit down
together and eat.
one Thing i enjoy about my country is
every Sunday wg go to Church on sunday
No Work.

I like The U.S. because i get
help with my education.
my comeing to the Us is a bless to i and
my Family. I like every thing about tis
country. Thanks to the U.SA.

Elizabeth,
        It is good to have
things about Liberia and the
U.S. that you like.
you are doing so well with
    your education !

Plus

Dialogue Journals

A dialogue journal is an informal written conversation between two or more people (student–student or student–teacher) about topics of mutual interest. These written conversations reinforce learning while forming bonds between students that can provide a foundation for later cooperative learning activities.

4) Authenticity

Authentic writing is those that reflect writing activities that are performed in real life outside the class such as: writing telephone message, texting on the phone, writing facebook messages, etc.

Another way of looking at authenticity issue is to distinguish between *real* writing and *display* writing. Real writing aims to get genuine communications with the readers: letters, e-mails, diaries, messages. On the other hand, display writing aims to display one's knowledge. Short answer, grammar exercises, essays and reports display writing skills and techniques.

5) Integrating ICT into English Writing Lesson

Example

Happy Thanksgiving!

Teaching Procedure

1. In a computer lab, the teacher places students in groups of three and asks them to search the Internet for information about how Americans celebrate Thanksgiving. The teacher recommends two or three pre-researched sites.

2. Students read the information on the sites, find three ways Thanksgiving differs from Chuseok, and then write a paragraph describing them in English.

3. Students then find two or three images on the Internet that support the differences they will show.

4. Students post their paragraphs and images on the class webpage bulletin board.

5. Once students have posted, they must then comment on other groups' posts.

6. As the students post, the teacher monitors the posts and gives feedback on each.

Memo

Chapter
03

Vocabulary and Grammar

Vocabulary and Grammar

01 \ Teaching Vocabulary

1 Current Approach

현재 어휘 지도는 개별 어휘의 형태와 뜻의 1 : 1 대응을 바탕으로 했던 과거의 어휘 지도에서 벗어나 <u>문맥 속의 어휘 덩어리(lexical chunk)를 바탕</u>으로 한 유의미한 학습으로 나아가고 있다. 실제 어휘에 대한 부담은 과업의 난이도로 연결된다. 대부분의 교사들은 실제로 학생들이 읽기에 대한 어려움에 부딪히게 된다고 언급하는데, 그것은 읽기 전략 때문이 아니라 어휘에 대한 충분한 지식을 갖추고 있지 않기 때문이라는 것을 깨닫게 된다.

Current vocabulary learning is more than the study of individual words. English language is made up of lexical phrases, which range from phrasal verbs to longer institutionalized expressions. Thus, *vocabulary load is the most signigicant predictor of text difficulty.* Most teachers says that the most significant handicap for especially reading comprehension is not lack of reading strategies but insufficient vocabulary in English. Students, also, point out lack of adequate vocabulary as one of the obstacles to text comprehension.

따라서, 현재 교실 수업의 어휘 지도는 양적으로 개별 어휘 수(breadth or size)를 늘려나가던 과거의 방식과는 다르게 진행돼야 할 것이다. 즉, 학습자의 수준에 맞춰 학습하고 기존 어휘의 질(depth or quality)을 높이는 데 주력해야 할 것이다. 요컨대 해당 어휘의 표면적 의미를 뛰어넘어 그 어휘의 발음, 철자, 통사 및 형태론적인 특징, 발화역(register), 동의어(synonymy), 다의어(polysemy), 병치어(collocation) 등의 정보를 익혀야 실질적인 어휘 활용(use)이 가능하다는 것이다.

03

In recent decades, there is a clear consensus that vocabulary knowledge comprise two dimensions, which are <u>vocabulary breadth, or size, and depth, or quality, of knowledge.</u> *Vocabulary breadth* refers to the number of words the meaning of which a learner has at least some superficial knowledge. *Depth of vocabulary knowledge* is defined as a learner' level knowledge of various aspects of a given word, or how well the learner knows this word. That is, *depth of knowledge focuses on the idea that for useful higher-frequency words learners need to have more than just a superficial understanding of the meaning*: it covers such components as pronunciation, spelling, meaning, register, frequency, and morphological, syntactic, and collocational properties.

(1) **How many words do our learners need to know?**

단어를 많이 알고 있는 것보다 얼마나 많은 핵심적인 단어(core words)—즉, 텍스트의 의미를 원활하게 파악해 주고 학생들의 이해를 돕는 데 필요한 어휘—를 알고 있는지가 더 중요하다고 볼 수 있다.

① **The ability of the same form to appear in many meanings (polysemy)**: Core words에 대한 정보를 많이 알수록 어휘력은 더욱 높아질 것이다. 가령, 'rich'라는 단어를 'having a lot of money'로 우선적으로 익히고 배우지만, 이것이 여러 맥락에서 상이한 의미로 사용되는 것을 알 수 있다. 'rich food, rich soil, rich in resources, a rich color' 등은 'money'와 그 어떤 관련 없이 다른 의미로 사용되는 것을 알게 되는 등 core words의 다양한 의미에 대한 이해는 깊이 있는 어휘 습득을 이끌어 낸다.

② **The ability of the same form to combine with other forms to make new meaning (collocation)**: Delexical verbs (have, take, do, etc.)는 동사 자체의 의미는 거의 가지고 있지 않으나, 다른 어휘 형태와 결합해 특정한 의미를 만들어 주며, 실제 빈번한 사용으로 이어진다. 가령, 'do'는 특별한 의미는 없으나, 특정한 명사와 연결되어 'do a favor, do a tour, do a lap, do the dishes, do the school run' 등의 새로운 의미로 사용된다.

(2) How words are organized and how we organize words

의미상 synonymy, antonymy, 그리고 hyponymy의 유형으로 조직해 학생들의 어휘력을 확대할 수 있다.

① 어휘상 대체 가능: start, begin / complete, end, and finish
② 의미상 반의어: wet-dry / light-dark, 단, 한 단어에 여러 가지 의미가 주어질 경우 주의해야 한다.

Example

> The opposite of rough could be of antonyms depending on the context.
>
> a. The surface is very *rough (smooth)*.
> b. Kyle was a very *rough (gentle)* child.
> c. The sea is *rough (calm)*.
> d. It was a *rough (accurate)* calculation.
> e. He had a very *rough (soft)* voice.

맥락 안에서(in context) 동의어(synonyms)와 반의어(antonyms)를 지도해야 한다. 이와 같은 지도가 이뤄지지 않을 경우, 학생들은 다양한 의미로 쓰이는 어휘를 한 의미로 과도하게 일반화를 시켜 오류를 생성할 수 있다(overgeneralization of meaning).

③ 위계적 분류(hierarchical categories): 'Water is a hyponym of liquid.'
'X는 Y의 한 형태이다.'를 보여주는 어휘들, 즉 mansion-house, sandal-shoe, barret-hat과 같이 의미를 토대로 어휘 학습을 지도할 경우 학생들의 어휘 확장을 도울 수 있으며, 특히 학생들이 알고 있는 어휘와 관련해 지도함으로써 어휘에 대한 retention을 높일 수 있다.

2 Explicit vs. Implicit Learning

어휘 습득은 수업 시간에 명시적으로 진행하는 방법과 다양한 읽기나 듣기 등을 통해 묵시적으로 진행하는 방법이 있다. 일반적으로 명시적인 지도를 통해 학습된 어휘가 묵시적인 습득으로 확대되는 것이 효과적이다.

Various researchers have concluded that learners should be given explicit instruction and practice in the first two to three thousand high-frequency words (i.e., word families), while beyond this level, most low-frequency words will be learned incidentally while reading or listening. A two or three thousand word base is considered a minimum "threshold" that enables incidental learning to take place when reading authentic texts.

(1) Intentional Learning

학습하는 어휘에 직접적인 관심(direct attention)을 두거나 어휘 습득에 초점을 둔 활동으로 학습자들이 어휘에 대한 학습을 하고 있음을 인식하게 된다. 어휘에 관한 지식이 낮은 초급 수준의 학습자들에게는 명시적인 어휘 지도가 보다 효과적이다. 이 경우 학습자들에게 우선적으로 필요한 common vocabulary, high frequency vocabulary를 토대로 이미 알고 있는 어휘를 정교화하는 학습 방법이 필요하다.

In explicit vocabulary learning students engage in activities that focus attention on vocabulary. There are several key principles of explicit learning that can help guide teachers in deciding basic questions of what to teach and how to teach. These principles include the goal of building a large recognition vocabulary, integrating new words with old, providing a number of encounters with a word, promoting a deep level of processing, facilitating imaging, using a variety of techniques, encouraging independent learning strategies. Here are two principles:

① **What to teach**: 얼마나 많은 어휘를 가르쳐야 하며, 어떤 어휘를 가르쳐야 할 것인지가 중요하다.

　ⓐ Productive vocabulary를 기준으로 high frequency words를 지도해야 한다. 즉, 빈번하게 노출되는 common vocabulary를 중심으로 지도하도록 한다.

　ⓑ 개별적인 어휘보다 word families 등을 토대로 지도하도록 한다. Word family는 base word에 inflections나 derivations 등이 포함된 어휘—talk, talked, talking, talks—들을 말한다. 즉, 4개의 다른 어휘가 아닌 하나의 'family'로 인지하고 학습하도록 한다.

② **Teaching techniques and activities**: 새로운 어휘 학습 시, 기계적인 학습 대신 다양한 맥락 안에서 어휘가 노출되고 의미에 대한 clue가 제공될 때 한 단어의 다양한 의미나 쓰임새를 효과적으로 학습할 수 있다. 가령, 관련 어휘 목록 만들기, 읽기 자료에 강조된 단어 주목하기(input enhancement), 단어 게임과 컴퓨터를 이용한 어휘 지도 활동 등 다양한 명시적 활동이 교실 수업에서 이뤄질 수 있다.

New words should not be presented in isolation and should not be learned by simple rote memorization. It is important that new vocabulary items be presented in contexts rich enough to provide clues to meaning and that students be given multiple exposure to items they should learn. Exercises and activities include learning words in word association lists, focusing on highlighted words in texts, and playing vocabulary games. More recently, computer programs that include the sounds of the words as well as illustrative pictures provide opportunity for practice with a variety of contexts, both written and spoken.

ⓐ **Semantic mapping**: An activity that helps bring into consciousness relationship among words in a text and helps deepen understanding by creating associative networks for words. A text is chosen based on the words to be learned and students are asked to draw a diagram of the relationships between particular words, found in the text.

ⓑ **Word association activities**: Constructed with lists of words that are to be learned. For example, students could be given word-match lists such as the following and asked to draw lines from words in the left column to those that seem most closely related in the right column.

Ex		
cough •		• pepper
grass •		• blue
red •		• tea
salt •		• kitten
puppy •		• sneeze
coffee •		• green

ⓒ **Word family**: Simply to introduce such a family along with the definitions for each word, as for example, the derivational set act, action, active, actively, activate, actor. Another way to isolate the word families that occur in a particular text is by highlighting them so that students can see the relationships. Highlighting passages in texts has the advantage of providing a more natural context in which students can trace words through the discourse and observe how the forms change according to discourse functions.

> Ex A *conductor* of an orchestra must spend years studying music and must also learn how to *conduct* other musicians so they can play together. The proper *conduct* of each musician will contribute to the success of the performance.

(2) Incidental Learning

수업 시간에 어휘가 아닌 다른 언어 기능을 습득하는 과정 혹은 학습자들이 다양한 읽기나 듣기를 하면서 어휘에 노출되는 과정에서 무의식적으로 어휘가 습득되는 경우를 말한다.

Incidental vocabulary learning is learning that occurs when the mind is focused elsewhere, such as on understanding a text or using language for communicative purpose. Explicit learning is thought to be necessary in the initial stages is that, unless a high percentage of words on a page are known, it is very difficult to guess that meaning of new words from context. Just as having multiple exposure to a word is important in explicit learning, so it is important for incidental learning. Lack of exposure is a common problem facing language learners; a good way to combat this problem is to expose students to extensive reading, sometimes referred to as a "book flood" approach, in which reading is done consistently over a period of time.

① **From controlled to automatic processing in a language classroom**: 제2언어 학습 과정에서 학습자들은 점차적으로 통제적인 언어 수행에서 자동적인 언어 수행을 보이게 된다. 즉, 명시적이고 구체적인 학습을 통해 길러진 선언적 지식(declarative knowledge)이 교실에서 일어나는 다양한 의미 있는 연습(meaningful practice)을 통해 절차적 지식(procedural knowledge)으로 전환되는 것이다. 따라서 교사는 학생들에게 교실 수업에서 명시적인 어휘 지도를 하고, 교실에서 다양한 어휘 학습 활동을 접하면서 해당 어휘를 실제 사용할 수 있는 능력으로 전환할 수 있도록 도와야 한다.

Example

Learning a second language(L2) may be viewed as the gradual transformation of performance from controlled to less controlled. This transformation has been called proceduralization or automatization and entails the conversion of declarative knowledge into procedural knowledge. According to this argument, the learning of skills is assumed to start with the explicit provision of relevant declarative knowledge and, through practice, this knowledge can hopefully convert into ability for use. At the same time, it is important to understand that learning an L2 may proceed in a different way. For example, some have wondered if incidental L2 learning is possible as a consequence of doing something else in the L2. Simply put, the question is about the possibility of learning without intention. The answer is still open, but, at present, it appears that people learn faster, more and better when they deliberately apply themselves to learning.

Mr Lee's Teaching Log

Through my teaching experience, I've learned that different students learn in different ways. Considering the current trend in teaching and learning, I believe that students should be provided with more opportunities to be exposed to the **incidental** learning condition. Minsu's case may illustrate that point. At the beginning of the semester, Minsu introduced himself as a book lover. He wanted to read novels in English but was not sure if he could. I suggested that he didn't have to try to comprehend all the details. Indeed, Minsu has benefitted a lot from reading novels. He said he learned many words and expressions even though he did not make attempts to memorize them. I will continue observing his progress as his way of learning is of great interest.

② Incidental vocabulary learning for level-differentiated students: 초급자들은 학습된 어휘를 중심으로 반복해서 학습할 수 있도록 graded readers를 활용해 어휘에 대한 노출을 극대화할 수 있고, 중급자에게는 동일한 토픽의 실제 자료(authentic texts)를 가급적 많이 제공해 토픽과 관련한 어휘에 대한 반복적인 노출을 진행함으로써 어휘 학습을 가속화할 수 있다. 반면에 상급자들은 다양한 실제 자료(authentic texts)를 접하도록 해 어휘에 대한 다양한 노출과 유형들을 파악하도록 함으로써 어휘력을 키워 나가도록 한다. 이와 같이 서로 다른 상황에서 동일한 어휘를 반복적으로 접함으로써 해당 어휘를 활용하고 지식을 확장시킬 수 있으며, 보다 견고하게 습득할 수 있게 된다.

For beginning students, graded readers will probably give the best access to a large amount of input. Also, they can benefit from graded readers because they will be repeatedly exposed to high frequency vocabulary. For intermediate students just on the threshold of reading authentic texts, it may be appropriate to read numerous authentic texts, but all the same topic (narrow reading) so that the texts will provide multiple exposure as topic-specific vocabulary is repeated throughout. Advanced students, on the other hand, should be encouraged to read a wide variety of authentic texts (wide reading). This type of exposure is important because meeting a word in different contexts expands what is know about it, thus improving quality of knowledge, with additional exposures helping to consolidate it in memory. Most words are probably learned incidentally through extensive reading and listening.

Plus ➕

It may be initially useful to devote some class time to Sustained Silent Reading for many students who may never have done extensive reading for pleasure. Once students develop the ability to read in a sustained fashion then most of the reading should be done outside of class.

3 Vocabulary Strategies

(1) **Guessing Strategies** – How to determine the meaning of unknown word

단어 자체의 품사, 병치어(collocation), 어휘가 쓰인 절(clause), 문장(sentence) 등의 맥락(context)을 통해서 어휘의 의미를 추측할 수 있다.

① Help students learn to recognize clues to guessing word meaning (low frequency vocabulary) from context; Provide rich authentic texts with enough adequate clues.

② Give opportunities for repeated encounters with a word in diverse context.

③ Encourage students to utilize their background knowledge about topic and the culture to infer the word meaning and to incorporate the new word with information already known.

In the Classroom

T : Today we are going to read some sentences. There are some unfamiliar words. We are going to try to figure out the meaning of the unfamiliar words by using clues that are around the words. All right, Cindy, please read the first one.

S1: The grandmother found some cherries, figs, apples, and pears on the table.

T : Does anyone know what figs are?

S2: Fruit.

T : *How did you know?*

S2: *Well everything else in the list is fruits, so it made sense that figs would be, too.*

T : Excellent. You used context clues or the words around figs to figure out that figs are a fruit. All right, Neil, please read the next one.

S3: She found a dove next to the fruit.

T : Very good sounding out of the word dove. Does anyone know what a dove is? (*The students shake their heads NO.*) Let's see if we can figure it out.

S4 : It is a toy.

T : No, John, it isn't a toy. Let's read the sentence again together.

Ss : She found a dove next to the fruit.

T : Do you have any ideas?

S2 : A knife.

T : Why do you think a knife?

S2 : So that she can cut the fruit.

T : An excellent guess. It is always good to guess. However, let me tell you something important. This is an example of a time when context won't help you. There isn't enough information in the sentence to figure out the meaning of the unfamiliar word.

(2) Vocabulary Analysis

단어의 의미를 모를 때는 해당 어휘를 분석하는 것도 좋은 전략이다.

① Look for *prefixes* (co-, inter-, un-, etc.) that may give clue.

② Look for *suffixes* (-tion, -tive, -ally, etc.) that may indicate what part of speech it is.

③ Look for *roots* that are familiar (e.g. 'intervening' may be a word a student doesn't know, but recognizing that the root 'ven' comes from Latin 'to come' would yield the meaning 'to come in between').

4 Classroom Techniques

(1) Keyword Method

Keyword method는 목표어와 비슷한 철자나 발음을 가진 모국어와 연결시키거나 이미지와 단어를 연결시켜 단어를 암기하는 방법이다.

The keyword method is called a "mnemonic device", which helps to link a word form and its meaning and to consolidate this linkage in memory. There are three stages.

① The learner chooses L1 and L2 word, preferable a concrete entity, based on a phonological or orthographic similarity with the target word.

② Strong association between the target word and the keyword must be constructed so that, when seeing or hearing the target word, the learner is reminded immediately of the keyword.

③ A visual image is constructed to combine the referents of the keyword and the target word, preferably an odd or bizarre image that will help make it more memorable.

(2) Word Map

Word maps are an extremely engaging way of building up vocabulary knowledge as well as provoking students into retrieving and using what they know.

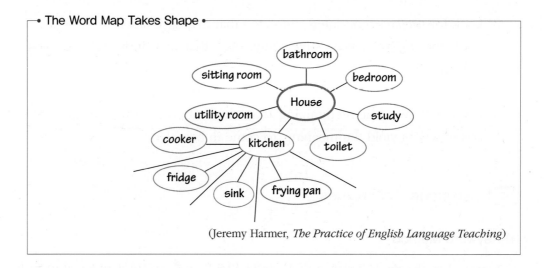

• The Word Map Takes Shape •

(Jeremy Harmer, *The Practice of English Language Teaching*)

(3) Concordance Program

Lexical approach와 함께 주목받기 시작한 concordance program은 방대한 어휘 목록에서 해당 어휘가 쓰인 문장만을 불러내어 어휘의 의미뿐 아니라 해당 어휘의 collocation이나 usage까지 학습할 수 있다.

Example ❶

Frequencies of the verbs let, allow and permit in spoken and written English

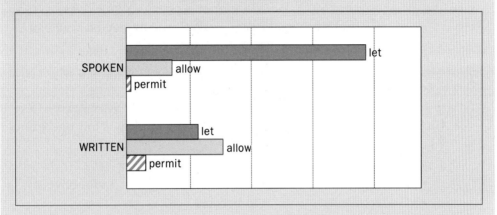

Based on the British National Corpus and the Longman Lancaster Corpus

This graph shows that *let* is much more common in spoken English than *allow* and *permit*. Allow is more common in written English. *Permit* is a formal word meaning to officially let someone do something.

(Longman Dictionary of Contemporary English)

Example ❷

Key Word: get

... Normally I	get	home by four o'clock ...
... s? You can	get	them in other shops ...
... at! Go and	get	your coat then. okay ...
... girl. she	gets	up off the ground ...
... My tea is	getting	cold. What's it ...
... Have you	got	any money on you? Not ...
... Anyway, I	got	this lovely letter ...
... well. He's	got	three children too ...

(British National Corpus (Spoken))

1. Look at the forms of get above with another student. Find one example where:
   a. *get* means
   - to buy
   - to arrive
   - to receive
   - to collect/fetch
   - to become
   b. *get + preposition* shows movement.
   c. *have + got* is used to talk about
   - possessions
   - family relations
   d. *got* is the Past Simple form of get.

(Mohamed S, and Acklam R, The Intermediate Choice, Longman)

Plus ✚

Vocabulary Teaching Principles in a Language Classroom

오늘날 내용과 과제 그리고 상호작용을 중시하는 의사소통 교수법이 대두됨에 따라, 어휘에 대한 새로운 관심이 일고 있다. 즉, 어휘 항목들을 암기하고 정의해야 하는 일련의 길고 따분한 단어 목록으로 여기지 않고, 언어를 유의미하게 만들고, 문맥화시키는 데 있어 중심적 역할을 수행하는 것이라고 본다.

1. 일부 수업 시간을 어휘 학습에 할애하라(Allocate specific class time to vocabulary learning).

상호작용적 수업을 진행하다 보면 자칫 어휘 학습에 별다른 관심을 기울이지 않을 수 있다. 어휘라는 것은 언어를 구성하는 가장 기본적인 단위이다. 그리고 초급 단계에서는 문법을 무시하고 단어만 배열하더라도 얼마간의 의사소통이 가능하다. 따라서 의사소통 능력 향상을 위해서는 가장 우선적으로 어휘 학습이 이뤄져야 할 것이다.

2. 학습자들로 하여금 문맥 속에서 어휘를 학습하도록 도와줘라(Help students to learn vocabulary in context).

문맥 속에서 어휘를 학습할 때 해당 어휘를 가장 효과적으로 내재화시킬 수 있다. 즉, 단어를 개별적으로 학습하거나 사전에 제시된 정의를 암기하는 것이 아니라, 해당 어휘가 등장하는 의사소통적 문맥 속에서 어휘를 학습하도록 장려해야 할 것이다. 그렇게 하면, 학습자들은 새로운 단어를 유의미한 상황과 연계시켜 이해하게 된다.

3. 영한사전의 사용을 억제하라(Play down the role of bilingual dictionaries).

학습자들은 새로운 단어가 나오면 문맥 속에서 이해하는 것이 아니라, 곧바로 영한사전(bilingual dictionary)을 찾아보는 경향이 있다. 이런 방식의 어휘 학습을 통해서는 해당 단어를 효과적으로 내재화시킬 수 없고, 후에 기억해 사용하는 데도 도움을 주지 못한다.

4. 학습자들로 하여금 단어의 의미 추론 전략을 개발하도록 장려하라(Encourage students to develop strategies for determining the meaning of words).

　Ex　Guessing Meaning from the Context

　　　다양한 단서들(접두사, 접미사, 동의어, 반의어 등)을 활용해 문맥 속에서 해당 어휘의 의미를 추론하는 전략을 개발하도록 장려해야 한다.

5. '계획되지 않은' 어휘 지도를 실시하라(Engage in 'unplanned' vocabulary teaching).

대부분의 경우 어휘 지도는 즉흥적으로 실시된다. 즉, 학생이 특정 어휘의 의미를 물어보거나, 학습 활동 속에서 등장한 특정 어휘를 다룰 필요가 있다고 판단되는 경우, 어휘 지도가 실시되는 것이다. 이러한 즉흥적인 어휘 지도는 매우 중요하다. 때때로 즉흥적인 어휘 지도를 확장시켜 여러 가지 예를 제시하거나 다른 문장 속에서 해당 어휘를 사용하도록 장려할 수도 있다. 단, 즉흥적 어휘 지도에 너무 많은 시간을 할애해 본시 학습 활동에 영향을 주면 안 될 것이다.

02 \ Teaching Grammar

의사소통 접근법에서 언어 사용의 문제점이 부각될 때, 인지적 접근법에서 주장하는 문법 학습의 필요성과 당위성이 보다 명확하게 드러난다. 이에 따라 현 접근법에서 언어를 가장 잘 학습할 수 있는 방법은 교실 수업이나 교실 밖에서 언어를 학습 대상으로 보되, 동시에 의사소통을 위한 수단으로써 유의미하게 사용하도록 하는 것이다. 즉, 'focus on form' approaches에서 주장하듯이 의사소통 과업 안에서 외형적으로 target forms를 부각시키거나 target forms가 포함된 활동을 하도록 하는 것이다.

The usefulness of a cognitive approach to grammar instruction in EFL becomes clear when we consider the problems with purely communicative approaches. The best way to learn a language, either inside or outside a classroom, is not by treating it as an object for study but by experiencing it meaningfully, as a tool for communication—perhaps with target grammar structures physically highlighted or embedded within communicative activities as recommended by current "focus-on-form" approaches to grammar instruction.

1 Meaning-focused and Form-focused Activities

일반적으로 교실에서 진행되는 대표적 교실 활동은 의미에 초점을 두는 의사소통 연습인 meaning-focused와 담화 맥락 안에서 언어 형태에 초점을 두는 언어 연습 활동인 form-focused로 나뉜다. 현 교수와 학습 측면에서는 목표 언어의 유창성과 정확성을 함께 기를 수 있도록 meaning-focused와 form-focused 활동들을 모두 진행할 필요가 있다. 따라서, 현 교실 수업에서는 의사소통 구조 안에서 일련의 문법 수업을 포함시켜 진행하는 접근법이 사용되고 있다.

There are two-types of classroom activities: 'meaning-focused', referring to purely communicative practice where the goal is to process meaning, and 'form-focused' referring to practices that draw attention to the way language forms are used in discourse. Both meaning-focused and form-focused activities are thought to be necessary for the successful development of both fluency and accuracy in foreign language learning. The value of meaning-focused communicative activities that provide learners with comprehensible input (also called "positive evidence") and opportunities to improve and correct their own output through interaction with others has been demonstrated repeatedly. However, form-focused activities emphasizing the features of particular grammar points are also necessary in order for learners to develop accuracy. Such activities range from indirect approaches to grammar instruction, such as the focus-on-form activities mentioned above, to traditional formal instruction where students are presented with grammar rules, examples, and practice exercises. Such form-focused approaches have been found to be effective in developing the learner's ability to use grammar forms communicatively if instruction is then followed by opportunities to encounter the instructed grammar point frequently in communicative usage.

03

Plus ➕

Approach to FFI (Form-focused Instruction)

1. Focus on Forms

과거에 문법 지도가 진행됐던 방식으로, 정확성에만 초점을 두고 문법 지도를 실시한다. 의사소통 상황과 문법 지도를 연계시키지 않고 탈맥락화(decontextualization)된 문법 학습이 일어난다.

2. Focus on Form

현재 의사소통 접근법에 가장 부합하는 문법 지도 접근법으로, 의미에 제1의 초점(meaning, first)을 두고 그 다음으로 정확성에 초점(form, second)을 두게 된다. 하지만 언어의 의미와 정확성 모두에 초점을 둔다는 점에서 focus on meaning과 focus on forms approach의 문법 지도와는 큰 차이가 있다.

Focus on form refers to the practice of explicitly drawing students' attention to linguistic features within the context of meaning-focused activities. In other words, communication comes first, and a focus on form comes second. The advantage of this reorientation is that "learner's attention is drawn precisely to a linguistic feature as necessitated by a communicative demand." Learners are therefore more likely to see the relationship between language form and communicative function.

➡ **Implication**: Teachers should present the grammar in a context that makes clear the relationship between the grammatical form and the communicative function.

Plus ⊕

1. Negative Evidence

언어 사용 시 학생들이 오류를 범해 교사나 동료 학생들로부터 해당 오류에 대한 설명이나 수정에 관련한 피드백을 받게 될 경우, 이를 'negative evidence'로 인지하고 오류 수정이 이뤄진다. 이와 같은 negative evidence는 학생들로 하여금 정확한 언어 형태에 대해 주목하게 하고, form—meaning의 관계를 형성하도록 하며, self—correction에 대한 요구(push)를 받게 돼 언어의 accuracy를 키워주도록 돕는다.

When students produce utterances with errors, if they receive corrective feedback from teachers/peers explaining the correct use of the form, or if the teacher/peer "recasts" or repeats the utterance so that the correct form is used, such error correction can provide "negative evidence," thereby facilitating learners' noticing of the correct form. In addition, *error correction can encourage students to build form—meaning relationships and, through self—correction, to "push" their output further in the direction of improved accuracy.* In fact, the learner's production of output—particularly when the output has been successfully corrected as the result of feedback from others—can then serve as new input. (successful uptake)

2. The Teachability Hypothesis

언어 습득에 있어서 자연적으로 미리 결정되는 보편적인 언어 습득 순서가 정해져 있디는 촘스키의 입장과 밀접한 관련을 지어 grammar instruction을 바라보고 있다. 따라서, *학생들이 습득에 대한 준비가 돼 있지 않으면 새로운 언어 구조를 습득하기 어렵다고 주장한다.* 하지만, 현재의 입장은 명확한 문법 학습과 언어 사용은 밀접한 관련이 있으므로 문법 학습이 필요하다는 입장을 취하고 있다.

"*Is there a set order for language development in the brain, in which case formal instruction may be ineffective if the student is not at the appropriate stage?*"

It proposes that second/foreign language learners will not acquire a new structure until they are developmentally ready to do so. If there were no connection between the development of explicit knowledge about a grammar point and the eventual restructuring of the unconscious linguistic system to accommodate the point in the learner's internal interlanguage, then, indeed, grammar instruction would not be of much use. However, it has been suggested that there is a connection, so grammar instruction is ultimately useful. Further, as the previous section emphasizes, practice of language points can lead to automatization, thus bypassing natural order/teachability considerations.

"*Learnability is the first consideration, and then comes the teachability.*"

2 Deductive vs. Inductive Approach

문법 지도에서 연역적인 접근법과 귀납적인 접근법은 상호 배타적인 관계가 아니라 학습자의 학습 스타일이나 교실 활동에 따라 적절히 혼용돼야 하는 상호 보완적인 관계 이다.

The deductive and inductive approaches are not mutually exclusive, and most teachers need to deploy both in their teaching.

(1) Deductive Approach(연역적인 접근법)

학습자들에게 먼저 규칙을 제시한 후 이 규칙을 주어진 예에 적용하도록 한다.

The teacher <u>presents the grammar rule</u> and then gives students exercises in which they <u>apply the rule.</u>

① rule-driven learning
② traditional grammar-translation approach
③ It gets straight to the point and can therefore be time-saving.
④ It may be frustrating for some students who do not have sufficient metalanguage.
⑤ a teacher-fronted and transmission style classroom

Example ❶

Sound the Same But Are Different!

> They're = They + are (Informal! No contractions in formal English)
> Their = belonging to or owned by two or more
> There = to talk about a place or location

Their love of music means that *they're* always going to concerts. *There* are many artists that they want to see live. Yesterday they went to pick up *their* Justin Timberlake tickets at the post office. But they weren't *there* yet. *They're* hoping to find them later.

Exercise

Choose a, b or c.

1. My friends are worried about_____ dog.
     a) their   b) there   c) they're

2. We'll worry about it when we get _____.
     a) their   b) there   c) they're

3. Were _____ any cookies left?
     a) their   b) there   c) they're

4. I borrowed _____ house for a few weeks.
     a) their   b) there   c) they're

(2) Inductive Approach(귀납적인 접근법)

학습자들에게 예를 먼저 제시하고 규칙을 찾아내도록 한다.

The teacher <u>presents samples of language</u>, and the students have to <u>infer the rule</u>.

① rule-discovery learning, more meaningful, memorable and serviceable
② direct method and natural approach
③ Students are more actively involved in the learning process.
④ Sometimes students may hypothesize the wrong rule or their version of the rule.

Example ❷

Sound the Same But Are Different!

Their love of music means that *they're* always going to concerts. *There* are many artists that they want to see live. Yesterday they went to pick up *their* Justin Timberlake tickets at the post office. But they weren't *there* yet. *They're* hoping to find them later.

Write your own rule for when to use *their, they're* or *there*:

Their is used to talk about _____.
They're is used _____.
There is used to talk about _____.

In the Classroom ||||||||||||||||||||||||||||||||||||||||||||||||||||||||||||||||||||||||||||||||||

03

1. Look at the chart. When do we use *does/doesn't*? When do we use *do/don't*?

Questions and Answers with do/does	
Do you know George?	Yes, I *do*.
Do they know your boss?	No, they *don't*.
Does he have glasses?	Yes, he *does*.
Does she wear earrings?	No, she *doesn't*.
Does he have curly hair?	No, he *doesn't*. He has straight hair.

2. Match the questions and answers. Then practice them with a partner.

① Do you know Lisa?   a. No, you don't.
② Does she have long hair?   b. Yes, they do.
③ Do they wear glasses?   c. No, he doesn't.
④ Does he have curly hair?   d. Yes, I do.
⑤ Do I know him?   e. No, she doesn't.

3. Fill in the missing information. Then ask your partner the questions.

① _____ your parents wear glasses?
② _____ you know my English teacher?
③ _____ you know my best friend?
④ _____ your best friend have curly hair?
⑤ _____ your best friend speak English?
⑥ _____ your sisters wear earrings?

Teacher A	Teacher B
T : OK, then. I want you to work in your pairs. Kevin, who's your partner? Jackie, is it? S : *(nods)* T : Good. OK, look at the questions and answer in the yellow box. I want you to practice the questions and answers in your pairs. OK? Kevin—Can you and Jackie do the first one for the class?	T : I want you all to look at the grammar box. What does it show us? Alice? S : About do/does. T : OK, good. I show you when we use the verb do/don't, does/doesn't in questions. Look at this table. *(Puts the following table on the board.)*

S : Do you know George?

S : Yes, I do.

T : OK. Excellent... So-off you go. *(Ss practice the questions and answers in pairs.)*

T : Everyone finished? Now, I'm going to ask some questions, and I want you to answer me. OK? Sharmy, do you know Kevin?

S : Yes, I do.

T : Kevin, do you wear earrings?

S : No, I don't.

T : How about Sharmy? Does she wear earrings?

S : Yes, she does.

T : Yes, she has great earrings, doesn't she? Um, Lillian, do you have curly hair?

S : Yes, I am.

T : Yes, I...?

S : Does... sorry... do.

T : Yes, I do. Good. OK. so... when do we use do/don't and when do we use does/ doesn't? *(Puts the following table on the board.)*

do/don't	does/doesn't
I, you, we, Sandra, your best friend	he, Erik and Amy, your boss, they

T : Some of these words are in the wrong box. Understand? Yes?

Ss : *(nod)*

T : OK, I want you to work with you partner. Copy the table, but put the words in the right box. Then see if you can add two more items to each box.

do/don't	does/doesn't
I, you, we, they George and kathi	he, Erik, she

T : Understand?

Ss : *(nod)*

T : OK, now I want you to look at Exercise B-matching the questions and answers. I want you to put a circle around all of the do and don't words you can find, and underline all of the does and doesn't words. OK? Understand?

Ss : *(nod)*

T : All right. And I want you to notice the pronouns they go with—I, you, he, she—maybe you can highlight them. OK? Right. Then I want you to match the questions with the right answers, and when you've done that, practice the questions and answers with your partner.

(3) Another Approach to Obtaining Linguistic knowledge – Abduction

① **Abduction**: Unlike inductive (i.e., data-driven, extracting rules and patterns from examples) and deductive (i.e., rule-driven, from rule-learning to rule application) reasoning, in abductive learning learners come to understand hidden rules of language use through the process of exploring hypothesis and inferences.

② **Abduction in the L2 classroom**

ⓐ **Step 1**: Present an authentic text that incorportates some features you want to highlight.

ⓑ **Step 2**: Design an activity that focuses on the target points: the target points into an information-gap activity.

ⓒ **Step 3**: Ask students work in groups and note the grammatical features or patterns they observe.

ⓓ **Step 4**: Students report their findings to the class.

③ **Expansion**

ⓐ **Step 5**: Inductive

ⓑ **Step 6**: Deductive

3 Explicit Grammar Instruction in Communicative Context

Example

Teaching Procedure

Step 1

The teacher asks students where they went last summer and what they took on their journey. Then she writes down the following sentences on the board and explains the difference in form and meaning between the two sentences using the terms 'past tense' and 'past participle(pp)'.

> I took a light jacket.
> I should have taken a warm jacket.

Step 2

The teacher hands out a story from a magazine that includes the target structure '**should** + **have** + **pp**'. She asks students to read the story carefully and look for the examples of '**should** + **have** + **pp**' in the given text.

> *Kate travelled across the Australian desert. She made no preparations. She didn't take a map, and she didn't take a cell phone. Soon after she set off, she got lost and got trapped in a flash flood. Later, looking back on it, she said, "I should have taken a map. I should have taken a cell phone..."*

Step 3

The teacher asks students to think about their own previous journey and complete the worksheet below.

Worksheet	
I _____ on my journey. *I should have _____ on my journey.*	I took a light jacket on my jacket on my journey. *I should have taken a warm journey.*

Step 4

The teacher asks students to write a story using the sentences they have produced in the worksheet above, and to share their writings with the partners.

Plus ➕

1. Explicit vs. Implicit Grammar Instruction

명시적(explicit)인 문법 지도에서는 규칙이 직접적으로 제시되기 때문에 학생들은 규칙을 한눈에 알 수 있다. 그러나 묵시적(implicit)인 문법 지도에서는 규칙이 직접적으로 제시되지 않고 주어진 언어적 자료에 암시돼 있다.

In explicit grammar instruction, grammar rules are clearly defined and explicitly stated. The rules are fully and clearly expressed and readily observable. On the other hand, implicit grammar instruction rejects the need for any kind or explicit focus on form. This is based on the belief that learners can acquire language naturally if they receive sufficient comprehensible input from the teacher. In implicit grammar instruction, the rules are implied or understood though not directly addressed and contained in the nature.

2. Declarative vs. Procedural Knowledge

선언적 지식(declarative knowledge)은 언어 규칙에 대해서 알고 규칙을 설명할 수 있는 지식을 말하는 데 반해 절차적 지식(procedural knowledge)은 의사소통을 위해 규칙을 사용하는 능력을 말한다.

Declarative knowledge is knowing language rules. *Procedural knowledge* is being able to use the knowledge for communication. Those who have *declarative knowledge* can state or explain the rule, but those who do not have *procedural knowledge* can not use the rule when using the language to communicate.

For example, the students who can tell that they have to put an *−s* on the end of the verb when making third person singular declarative statements have declarative knowledge, but not procedural knowledge.

While declarative knowledge can facilitate the development of procedural knowledge, it is not a necessary and sufficient condition for the development of such knowledge.

Activity A

Change the sentences as in the example, and check your answers with your partner. Then explain to your partner the grammatical rule(s) you applied.

a. I have been to New York several times.

⇒ I went to New York last month.

b. She has read the book before.

⇒ _____ a month ago.

c. We have known about the problem for ages.

⇒ _____ yesterday.

Activity B

In pairs, read the following conversation extracts, focusing on the parts in italics. What is the difference between what Person A and Person B say? When would you use one form or the other? Share your thoughts with your partner.

a. A: I'*ve won* a prize in the English−speaking competition.

B: Yeah? I *won* a prize in the poetry competition *last year*.

b. A: I'*ve seen* "Romeo and Juliet" *twice*.

B: Me, too. I *saw* it *last Tuesday* and again *on the weekend*.

c. A: A strange thing *happened* to me *yesterday*. I couldn't remember my cell phone number.

B: Really? That *has happened* to me *several times*, too.

---

④ 수업 활동

(1) Input Enhancement / Input Flooding

가르치고자 하는 구문이 많이 포함된 자료를 사용하거나 목표 구문의 크기와 색을 달리 하거나 밑줄을 그어 강조함으로써 학습자들의 의식(grammatical consciousness-raising)을 높인다.

Input enhancement is a technique for getting students to notice the grammar item that the teacher wants to introduce. With this technique, a teacher draws students' attention to items that are meant to be noticed *by highlighting, underlining, or coloring and by using materials that contain a lot of target items (input flooding)*.

> **Plus** ⊕
>
> **Noticing Hypothesis**
>
> 성공적인 언어 학습을 위해 학습자들에게 target form에 대한 noticing의 기회를 교실 수업에서 다양하게 제공해야 할 것이다. Noticing은 학습자에게 target form에 대한 즉각적인 습득을 이끌지는 않지만 습득으로 이어지는 시작점(essential starting point)이 될 것이다.
>
> According to Noticing Hypothesis, second language learners cannot begin to acquire a language feature until they have become aware of it in the input through noticing. The conscious cognitive effort of noticing is "a necessary and sufficient condition for the conversation of input to intake" in a second language acquisition. Noticing opportunities may be provided within communicative settings without teacher initiated focus. But in order for uptake to occur organically, the learner should be provided with plenty of meaningful input through authentic L2 materials. Providing opportunities for noticing is believed to be particularly important when salience of form is low. Prompting noticing opportunities can be a much more intentional process. An explicit form of noticing instructional techniques might include pointing specific forms out when supplying input that contains them or reaction to incorrect output through recasts.

(2) Input Processing

교사는 학습자들에게 목표 구문의 형태보다 목표 구문과 관련 있는 그림 등을 먼저 제시한다. 학생들은 형태보다 의미를 먼저 접한 뒤 형태와 의미를 결합하고 연관 지음으로써 구문을 학습하게 된다.

Input processing is an approach to grammar instruction that guides learners to process what they see or hear. This approach helps learners *connect language forms with their intended meanings*. Learners must DO something with the input they see or hear.

① Learners need structured input activities that enable them to focus on meaning while attending to form before they are expected to use the language to produce output.

② The goal of input processing instruction is to encourage learners to make better form-meaning connections than they would be if left to their own devices.

Example

Choose the sentence that goes with the picture.

ⓐ The man *bit* a snake.
ⓑ The man was *bitten by* a snake.

ⓐ The elephant *frightened* by the mouse.
ⓑ The elephant *was frightened by* the mouse.

ⓐ The mother *fed* the child.
ⓑ The mother *was fed by* the child.

1. Students are encouraged to match picture with italic-typed forms which carry the active and passive voice. In other words, a form-meaning relationship in the picture explains the use of the passive to topicalize the patient of a sentence by placing it in subject position.

2. The picture leads learners to attend to the form of the verb to determine whether the subject is the agent of the verb, as is most generally the case with active verbs, or the patient, as is the case with passive verbs.

3. The worksheet represents a structured-input activity where learners have the chance to process the target feature in a controlled manner. Unlike the traditional grammar instruction, this activity is designed to help learners naturally process input in accordance with their interlanguage.

Plus ✚

Traditional Approach & Input Processing Approach

1. Traditional Approach

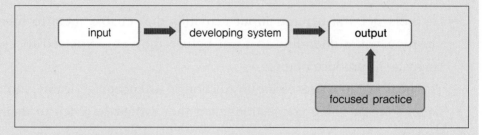

a. Learners see or hear input.
b. They think about it . . . (?)
c. They practice during output.

2. IP Approach

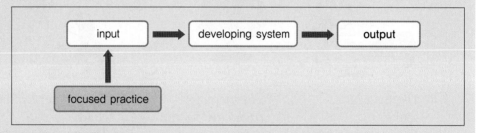

a. Learners see or hear input.
b. They DO something with what they see or hear.
c. They produce the word or structure.

(3) Consciousness-raising Tasks

학습자들에게 해당 규칙이 적용된 일련의 예들을 제공한 뒤 규칙을 도출하도록 하고 그 규칙을 자신의 상황에 맞게 적용 및 연습하는 단계로 이뤄진다.

Deductive means of teaching grammar tend to emphasize form over meaning, and promote passive rather than active participation of the learners in the learning process. Such approaches are believed to intimidate learners. Instead, awareness-raising inductive approach helps to develop learners' own understanding of language, and to build confidence in themselves as learners. Further, *allowing the learners to take responsibility for discovering target rules favorably affects retention*. Consciousness-raising tasks, which can be either deductive or inductive, offer an effective means of teaching grammar.

A CR task can be defined as a grammar activity where students are provided with L2 data in some form and required to perform some operation on or with it, the purpose of which is to arrive at an explicit understanding of some linguistic property or properties of the target language.

Example

Indirect Task for Relative Clauses: task sheet for student A

Student A

A. Look at the table below. The relative clauses are in italics, the prepositions are underlined and the relative pronouns are in bold.

B. You need to work with your partner to complete the table. Ask your partner to read out his/her sentences. Listen carefully, the write them down in the appropriate column in your table.

C. Talk about the sentences. Why are the sentences in the second column incorrect?

Complete the rules in the final column by filling in the blanks.

	Correct	Incorrect	Explanation of incorrect sentences
1	The place *to* **which** *you will want to go* is Singapore. The place **which** *you will want to go to* is Singapore. The man *at* **whom** *I shouted* is deaf. The man **whom** *I shouted at* is deaf.		Don't use prepositions both at the _____ and at the _____ of the clause.
2		The girl *to* **who** *we gave the message* is not here. The house *in* **that** *we live* is pink.	Don't use prepositions at the _____ of the clause.
3	These are the books **which** *I told you about.* The man **who** *you were talking to* is my uncle.		Don't use personal pronouns at the _____ of the clause.

D. Now write down a sentence of your own for each of these rules.

1. _____

2. _____

3. _____

Indirect Task for Relative Clauses: task sheet for student B

Student B

A. Look at the table below. The relative clauses are in italics, the prepositions are underlined and the relative pronouns are in bold.

B. You need to work with your partner to complete the table. Ask your partner to read out his/her sentences. Listen carefully, the write them down in the appropriate column in your table.

C. Talk about the sentences. Why are the sentences in the second column incorrect?

Complete the rules in the final column by filling in the blanks.

	Correct	Incorrect	Explanation of incorrect sentences
1		That is the person *from* **whom** *I got the letter from.* The book *in* **which** *you wrote in* is mine.	Don't use prepositions both at the _____ and at the _____ of the clause.
2	The girl **who** *we gave the message to* in not here. The house **that** *we live in* is pink.		Don't use prepositions at the _____ of the clause.
3		These are the books **which** *I told you about them.* The man **who** *you were talking to him* is my uncle.	Don't use personal pronouns at the _____ of the clause.

D. Now write down a sentence of your own for each of these rules.

1. _____

2. _____

3. _____

(4) Garden Path

교사는 학생들에게 목표 구조에 대한 부분적인 정보를 제공하고 규칙을 도출하도록 해 학습자들의 과잉일반화를 유도한다. 즉, 오류를 통한 문법에의 의식 상승을 도움으로써 학습자들은 더 유의미한 문법 학습을 할 수 있게 된다.

The teacher gives students information about structure without giving them the full picture. Then, students are asked to infer the rule from the partial information. This makes students overgeneralize and leads them into error. They are given disconfirming evidence and then have to modify their hypothesis.

① This is based on inductive learning.
② The reason for giving students only a partial explanation is that they are more likely to learn the exceptions than if they are given a long list of exceptions to the rule to memorize in advance.

5 Grammar-based Approach

(1) The Non-interface Position

Arguing in support of an innate mechanism called Language Acquisition Device(LAD) which is assumed to be responsible for both first and second language acquisition (i.e. L1=L2), Krashen posits that the structure of language is so complex that can be acquired only through a large amount of exposure to sufficient amount of comprehensible input (i+1) which focuses on meaning rather than form. Based on this, the central part of instruction should address developing implicit, meaning-based knowledge of language and no essential role is assigned to explicit knowledge of language forms. More specifically, explicit, conscious knowledge of grammatical forms (i.e. learning) can't convert into implicit, unconscious knowledge (i.e. acquisition). This dissociation of explicit knowledge from implicit knowledge has been referred to as the 'non-interface' position.

(2) The Strong Interface Position

Unlike the non-interface position which aimed at developing unconscious, implicit knowledge of L2, the strong interface position intended to promote Learned Linguistic Knowledge (Schwartz, 1993) which required learners to explicitly learn L2 forms. Simply put, it was assumed that that there is a direct interaction between explicit knowledge/learning and implicit knowledge/ learning and that L2 learning takes place with explicit focus-on-forms. Drawing upon the widely held belief that 'practice makes perfect', characterised as a *skill-learning theory*, most advocates of this position argued that learning L2 forms is best achieved through a *PPP* procedure: 1) Presenting the targeted structure through explicit instruction, 2) Practising the structure until it is followed by 3) Producing that structure.

(3) The Weak Interface Position

While in the strong interface position, explicit knowledge directly converts to implicit knowledge through plentiful practice, in the weak interface position explicit knowledge converts to implicit knowledge both directly and indirectly. Explicit knowledge directly changes to implicit knowledge through explicit rule presentation; besides, it is indirectly transformed to implicit knowledge through noticing (i.e. *attention to some specific features in the input*) and noticing the gap (i.e. *comparing the targeted features in the input with existing mental grammar*). The concept of 'noticing' has come to be known under different terms: consciousness-raising, focus on form, attention, awareness and input enhancement. The type of instruction based on this position is commonly known as the focus-on-form instruction. This approach to teaching grammar aims at drawing learners' attention to some specific linguistic form through saliency or frequency of that form during meaning-based instruction or when form-based problems incidentally arise in lessons whose overriding focus is on meaning or communication. So, it is claimed that both form and meaning, both explicit and implicit knowledge/learning and both accuracy and fluency are all simultaneously taken into account and that is how the criticisms against the former extremist positions are accommodated.

Memo

Chapter
04

Assessment

Assessment

구성주의 측면에서 평가는 교사와 학생 간의 상호작용으로 간주되며, 교사는 학생의 기존 지식을 토대로 평가해야 한다. 또한, 학생들의 언어능력을 향상시키도록 고안돼야 하며, 평가 기준이 명확하게 학생들에게 전달돼야 하고, 다양한 평가 방식을 통해 수행 능력을 평가해야 한다. 마지막으로, 학생들은 평가 방식에 대한 (특히 익숙지 않은 평가 유형에 대한) 연습 및 훈련의 기회를 가져야 하며, 평가 결과는 즉각적으로 학생들에게 제공해 결과에 대한 토의가 이뤄져야 한다.

A more constructive view of language testing exists when ① testing is seen as an opportunity for interaction between a teacher and students, ② students are judged on the basis of the knowledge they have, ③ the tests are intended to help students improve their skills, ④ the criteria for success on the test are clear to students, ⑤ students receive a grade for their performance on a set of tests representing different testing methods (not just one), ⑥ the test takers are trained in how to take tests—especially those involving unfamiliar formats, ⑦ the tests are returned promptly, and ⑧ the results are discussed.

01 \ Principles of Assessment

1 Practicality

평가는 실용적(practical)이어야 한다. 실용적인 평가는 재정적 한계와 시간적 제약 속에서도 실시할 수 있어야 하며, 평가 채점 및 해석이 용이해야 한다.

An effective test is practical. That means the practical test is not excessively expensive, stays within appropriate time constraints, is relatively easy to administer, and has a scoring/evaluation procedure that is specific and time-efficient.

2 Reliability

신뢰도 있는 평가는 서로 다른 상황에서 실시해도 유사한 결과가 나오는 평가를 말한다. 즉 신뢰도 있는 평가는 유사한 학습자를 대상으로 다시 실시해도 그 결과가 일관성이 있어야 한다.

Reliability is defined as the degree to which a test gives consistent and dependable results. Sources of unreliability may lie in the test itself or in the scoring of the test known as test reliability and rater (or scorer) reliability.

(1) 채점자 간 신뢰도(Inter-rater Reliability)

둘 이상의 채점자가 채점을 할 경우 불확실한 채점 기준, 선입견, 부주의 등에 의해 평가 신뢰도가 낮아질 수 있다.

Two or more scorers yield inconsistent scores of the same test, possibly for lack of attending to scoring criteria, inexperience, inattention, or even preconceived biases.

(2) 채점자 개인 신뢰도(Intra-rater Reliability)

한 명의 채점자가 채점을 하더라도 불확실한 채점 기준, 장시간의 채점, 선입견 등에 의해 신뢰도는 낮아질 수 있다.

A common occurrence of low intra-rater reliability results from unclear scoring criteria, fatigue, biases toward particular students, or simple carelessness.

Example

> When I am faced with up to 40 tests to grade in only a week, I know that the standards I apply—however subliminally—to the first few tests will be different from those I apply to the last few. I may be 'easier' or 'harder' on those first few papers or I may get tired, and the result may be an inconsistent evaluation across all tests.
>
> ➡ 채점자 개인의 신뢰도를 높이기 위해 위와 같은 상황에서는 전체 시험에 대한 채점을 하기 전 절반 정도를 먼저 살피고 대략적인 채점 기준을 설정한 후 처음으로 돌아가 정해진 기준으로 채점을 진행해야 한다.

3 Validity

평가의 타당도란 측정하고자 하는 것을 제대로 측정하는가를 말한다. 평가가 학생들의 능력을 오차 없이 측정했더라도, 즉 신뢰도가 높더라도 평가 항목 자체가 측정하고자 하는 언어 기능이 아니라면 평가는 평가자에게 적절한 정보를 제공하지 못한다.

Validity is defined as the extent to which information you collect actually reflects the characteristic or attitude you want to know about. In other words, as assessment instrument such as a test is valid only if it tests exactly what it means to test.

(1) 내용타당도(Content Validity)

특정 평가가 측정하고자 하는 내용을 평가했다면 그 평가는 내용타당도를 지닌다고 할 수 있다. 교실 평가에서 내용타당도가 높으려면 학습한 내용으로 평가를 구성해야 한다.

Content validity is determined by checking the adequacy with which *the test samples the content or objectives of the course or area being assessed*. For the language teacher, the degree of test validity is derived from a meticulous analysis of the content of each item and of the test as a whole.

Example ❶

If you are trying to assess a person's ability to speak a second language in a conversational setting, asking the learner to answer paper-and-pencil multiple-choice questions requiring grammatical judgments does not achieve **content validity**.

Example ❷

다음은 초급자 말하기 활동반에서 진행된 영어 관사에 대한 퀴즈이다.

Directions: The purpose of this quiz is for you and me to find out how well you know and can apply the rules of article usage. Read the following passage and write a/an, the, or 0 (no article) in each blank.

Last night, I had ① _____ very strange dream. Actually, it was ② _____ nightmare! You know how much I love ③ _____ zoos. Well, I dreamt that I went to ④ _____ San Francisco zoo with ⑤ _____ few friends. When we got there, it was very dark, but ⑥ _____ moon was out, so we weren't afraid. I wanted to see ⑦ _____ monkeys first, so we walked past ⑧ _____ merry-go-round and ⑨ _____ lions' cages to ⑩ _____ monkey section.
(The story continues, with a total of 25 blanks to fill.)

➡ 학생들의 수업은 동물원의 동물들을 주제로 토의와 소집단 활동을 통한 말하기와 듣기 활동으로 관사 연습이 진행됐다. 본 수업을 마치고 제시된 위와 같은 퀴즈는 학생들에게 익숙한 내용과 수업에서 연습한 관사의 형태가 제시됐다는 점에서 *내용에 대한 타당도가 있다*고 볼 수 있다. 반면에 평가가 문어로 돼 있고, 해당 내용을 읽도록 하며 답 역시 쓰기로 진행된다는 점에서 *듣기와 말하기 수업에 관한 내용타당도는 낮다*고 볼 수 있다.

(2) 안면타당도(Face Validity)

안면타당도란 학습자가 평가를 봤을 때 학습자의 관점에서 해당 평가가 측정하고자 하는 것을 측정하는 것처럼 느끼는 정도를 말한다.

Face validity concerns about whether the test looks as if it is measuring what it is supposed to measure. That is the look of a test can influence the test taker. Conditions for high face validity:

① a well-constructed, expected format with familiar tasks

② a test that is clearly doable within the allotted time limit

③ items that are clear and uncomplicated

④ directions that are crystal clear

⑤ tasks that relate to their course work (content validity)

⑥ a difficulty level that presents a reasonable challenge

Example

I once administered a dictation test and a cloze test as a placement test for a group of learners of English as a second language. Some learners were upset because such tests, on the face of it, did not appear to them to test their true abilities in English. They felt that a multiple-choice grammar test would have been the appropriate format to use. A few claimed they didn't perform well on the cloze and dictation because they were not accustomed to these formats. As it turned out, the tests served as superior instruments for placement, but the students would not have thought so.

➡ 안면타당도가 매우 낮으나(low face validity), 구성타당도가 매우 높다(high construct validity).

(3) 구성타당도(Construct Validity)

구성타당도는 평가를 할 때 평가 목표 또는 평가 기준의 이론적인 구성(개념)을 배경으로 하고 있는지를 말한다. 예를 들어 의사소통 능력을 측정하고자 할 때 의사소통 능력을 구성하는 이론적인 개념인 조직적 능력, 화용적 능력, 전략적 능력 등을 모두 포함한 평가를 실시한다면 구성타당도가 높다고 할 수 있다.

Construct validity refers to the degree to which scores on an assessment instrument permit inferences about underlying traits. In other words, it examines whether the instrument is a true reflection of the theory of the trait being measured.

Example ❶

Oral Interview

The scoring analysis for the interview includes several factors in the final score: pronunciation, fluency, grammatical accuracy, vocabulary use, and sociolinguistic appropriateness. The justification for these five factors lies in a theoretical construct that claims those factors to be major components of oral proficiency. So if you were asked to conduct an oral proficiency interview that evaluated only pronunciation and grammar, you could be justifiably suspicious about the **construct validity** of that test.

Example ❷

Written Vocabulary Quiz

Likewise, let's suppose you have created a simple written vocabulary quiz, covering the content of a recent unit, that asks students to correctly define a set of words. Your chosen items may be a perfectly adequate sample of what was covered in the unit, but if the lexical objective of the unit was the communicative use of vocabulary, then the writing of definitions certainly fails to match a construct of communicative language use (Brown, 2004).

(4) 준거타당도(Criterion-related Validity)

시행된 평가 결과가 동일 능력을 측정하는 믿을 만한 다른 평가 결과와 비슷하다면 준거 타당도가 있다고 할 수 있다.

① 공인타당도(concurrent validity): 현재의 평가 결과가 기존의 타당성을 입증받고 있는 검사와 동일한지의 여부를 의미한다.

② 예측타당도(predictive validity): 어떤 평가에서 좋은 결과를 얻은 피험자가 이와 관련된 미래의 실제 생활에서도 성공적으로 그 능력을 수행하고 있다면 예측타당도가 높다고 할 수 있다.

④ Authenticity

목표 언어의 과업과 제시된 언어 평가 과업이 일치할 경우 혹은 실제 상황이나 실제 생활에 관련된 과업을 그대로 모사하는 경우 진정성(authenticity) 있는 평가라 할 수 있다.

Authenticity is defined as the degree of correspondence of the characteristics of a given language test task to the features of a target language task. For authenticity in a test, a task is likely to be enacted in the 'real world.' Thus, the sequencing of items that bears no relationship to one another lacks authenticity.

① The language in the test is as natural as possible.

② Items are contextualized rather than isolated.

③ Topics are meaningful, relevant, interesting for the learner.

④ Some thematic organization to items is provided, such as through a story line or episode.

⑤ Tasks represent, or closely approximate, real-world tasks.

Example

When I planned a listening test, I selected a conversation text from real-world sources that my students are likely to have encountered or will encounter. Listening comprehension sections feature natural language with hesitations, white noise, and interruptions.

Type A	Type B
"going to"	
1. What _____ this weekend?	1. There are three countries I would like to visit. One is Italy.

a. you are going to do
  b. are you going to do
  c. your gonna do
	a. The other is Japan and other is Nepal.
	  b. The others are Japan and Nepal.
	  c. Others are Japan and Nepal.

2. I'm not sure. _____ anything special?

  a. Are you going to do
  b. You are going to do
  c. Is going to do

3. My friend Melissa and I _____ a party. Would you like to come?

  a. am going to
  b. are going to go to
  c. go to

2. When Mr. Brown designs a website, he always creates it _____.

  a. artistically
  b. artistic
  c. artist

3. When Mona broke her leg, she asked her husband _____ her to work.

  a. to drive
  b. driving
  c. drive

➡ Type A의 각 항목들은 하나의 topic을 가지고 문항 간의 긴밀한 연계성을 토대로 유의미한 문맥을 이루고 있는 반면, B의 개별 항목들은 유의미하지만 항목 간 연계성이 없다. 따라서 A는 authenticity가 있지만 B의 항목들은 authenticity가 떨어진다.

5 Washback Effect

역류효과(washback effect)란 평가가 다음 학습에 미치는 영향으로, 긍정적인 것과 부정적인 것이 있으며 긍정적인 역류효과가 높아야 한다. 즉, 학생의 장단점에 대한 정보를 제공함으로써 내적 동기, 자신감, 언어적 자아, 언어 사용 전략 등을 높이도록 평가를 구성해야 한다.

A facet of consequential validity is the effect of testing on teaching and learning, known as "washback effect." It provides *the information that washes back to students in the form of useful diagnoses of strengths and weaknesses.*

Example

In my courses I never give a final examination as the last scheduled classroom session. I always administer a final exam during the penultimate session, then complete the evaluation of the exams in order to return them to students during the last class. At this time, the students receive scores, grades, and comments on their work, and I spend some of the class session addressing material on which the students were not completely clear. My summative assessment is thereby enhanced by some beneficial washback that is usually not expected of final examinations.

➡ 역류효과를 높이기 위해서는 학생이 자신의 수행 결과를 언제든 교사와 토의할 수 있는 창구를 마련해 줘야 한다.

Plus ➕

1. 긍정적인 역류효과를 이끌어 내기 위한 방법

① 내용타당도가 높은 평가

② 평가 전후의 전략으로 평가 전 준비와 평가 결과를 다음의 학습에 반영하도록 하는 경우

③ 대안평가 실시: self-assessment, freer discussion of the test results, journal writing 등

Ex A few years ago in a certain country there was a serious shortage of examiners who had any real degree of oral fluency in English. As a result, it was generally agreed that any oral interview test would be very unreliable indeed since many candidates were more fluent than the examiners.

Nevertheless, the examining body kept the oral interview test because it felt that no English at all would be spoken in the last year of the secondary school if the oral components were abolished! (negative washback effect을 차단하기 위해)

2. How to balance teaching and testing in an exam class

① **The weak class**: These students tend to lack essential knowledge and language skills, so the priority has to be teaching rather than testing. The aim is still to get them through the exam, but this is combined with a realistic assessment of their capabilities and a programme of teaching which recognizes their limitations and fills in the gaps in their basic knowledge of the language.

② **The average-to-good class**: These students have already covered all the basic language patterns and vocabulary and have reasonably well-developed skills, although writing is often weaker than their other skills, perhaps due to lack of pressure to practise. They still have plenty of work to do, but their need is to review and consolidate what they should already know. They also need to practice those skills, normally reading and writing, which tend to be more emphasized in exams than on non-exam courses. Regular testing should have the effect of proving to these students what they can achieve through steady hard work, and provide a positive challenge.

③ **The strong class**: They are already up to the required level, and there is not a lot to teach them beyond familiarization with the exam format and how to answer questions in the best way possible. This sort of class can sometimes be hard to motivate, since everything to do with the exam is quite easy for them. Teaching can concentrate on challenging them further in areas where they can demonstrate above-average ability, such as vocabulary range, stylistic sensitivity, and pronunciation and intonation. They can be shown how the marking criteria credit exceptional ability and how those who pass at the top level are distinguished from those who achieve an average pass.

04

02 \ 평가의 유형

1 형성평가와 총괄평가

(1) 형성평가(Formative Test)

학습자들이 학습 목표를 잘 성취하고 있는지 알아보고, 또 학습자들에게 필요한 다음 단계가 무엇인지 알아보기 위해 <u>수업 중 혹은 학기 중에 실시하는 평가</u>이다.

> **Ex** 수업 중 질문, 확인 작업, 중간고사, 월말고사

① evaluating students *in the process of "forming" their competencies and skills with the goal of helping them to continue that growth process*

② the delivery (by the teacher) and internalization (by students) of appropriate feedback on performance, with an eye toward the future continuation of learning

③ Virtually all kinds of informal assessment are formative. So when teachers give students *a comment or a suggestion, or call attention to an error, that feedback* is offered in order to improve the learner's language ability.

(2) 총괄평가(Summative Test)

학생들이 해당 <u>교육과정을 이수하고 난 뒤 해당 학습 목표를 잘 성취했는지 측정</u>하기 위한 평가로 계획적이고 체계적이다.

> **Ex** 기말시험, 학년말고사

① aiming to measure, or summarize what a student has grasped

② occurring *at the end of a course or unit of instruction*

③ Summation of what a student has learned implies looking back and taking stock of how well that student has accomplished objectives, but does not necessarily point the way to future progress.

④ *Final exams* in a course and general proficiency exams are examples of summative assessment.

2 직접평가와 간접평가

(1) 직접평가(Direct Testing)

측정하고자 하는 능력을 직접 수행하도록 지도해 이를 평가한다. 평가자가 즉각적인 피드백을 제공할 수 있기 때문에 교수·학습에 대한 긍정적인 역류효과(washback effect)가 크다.

> **Ex** 수행평가(formative test)

(2) 간접평가(Indirect Testing)

평가하고자 하는 능력을 간접적으로 평가한다.

> **Ex** 듣기평가에서 'What is the man's response to the last utterance?'라는 질문을 통해 말하기 능력을 간접적으로 측정하는 경우

3 객관식 평가와 주관식 평가

(1) 객관식 평가(Objective Testing)

선다형(multiple choice), 진위형(true or false), 문장 재배열하기, 연결하기(matching) 등이 해당되며, 타당도가 결여되기 쉽다.

(2) 주관식 평가(Subjective Testing)

서답형, 논술형이 해당되며, 채점이 쉽지 않고 신뢰도가 다소 떨어지지만 타당도가 높다.

4 상대평가와 절대평가

(1) 상대평가(Norm-referenced Testing)

한 피험자의 수행을 다른 피험자의 수행과 비교해 결과를 평가한다. 학습자들 사이에서의 상대적인 위치에 대한 정보를 얻을 수 있다.

(2) 절대평가(Criterion-referenced Testing)

피험자들이 학습 목표를 어느 정도 달성했는지에 대해서 다른 학생들 간의 비교 없이 절대적인 성취 정도를 평가한다.

5 분리평가와 통합평가

(1) 분리평가(Discrete-point Testing)

언어의 각 기능 요소들을 분리해 한 번에 하나의 항목을 평가하는 방식으로, 대부분의 *선다형이나 진위형 문제*가 이에 해당한다. 채점이 용이하고 객관적이어서 신뢰도가 높은 반면, 실제 의사소통 상황에서는 언어 기능들이 따로 사용되는 것이 아니기 때문에 언어 능력 평가에 대한 타당도가 낮다.

① behavioristic/structural approach to language learning and teaching in contrastive analysis

② *knowledge of specific elements in phonology, grammar, and vocabulary in order to determine proficiency in the isolated skill areas of listening, reading, speaking, and writing*

③ auditorially distinguishing between "pill" and "bill" or recognizing a past tense form or the present progressive

(2) 통합평가(Integrative Testing)

언이의 다양한 능력과 기능들을 한 번에 측정한다. 즉 하나의 평가 혹은 과업을 달성하는 데 동시에 둘 이상의 언어 능력을 필요로 하는 평가가 해당된다. 대표적인 통합평가로는 *dictation, cloze test* 등이 있다.

① developmentalistic/communicative approach

② examining the student's ability *to use many skills simultaneously when accomplishing a task*

③ answering the question relating to the conversation or writing an effective letter

03 \ 목적에 따른 평가의 분류

1 언어능력평가(Proficiency Test)

언어에 관련된 학습자의 전반적인 능력을 측정하는 것이다. 언어능력평가는 대부분 대규모 학생들을 대상으로 실시되는데, 대표적인 언어능력평가로는 TOEFL을 꼽을 수 있다.

We use proficiency tests to measure how suitable candidates will be for performing a certain task or following a specific course.

2 진단평가(Diagnostic Test)

언어능력의 특정 측면을 진단하기 위해 고안된 평가이다. 주로 특정 언어 수업을 시작하기 전에 학습자의 학습 전 능력을 진단하거나 학습 과정 중에 부족한 부분을 보충하기 위해 실시된다.

A good diagnostic test helps us to check our students' progress for *specific weaknesses and problems* they may have encountered.

3 배치평가(Placement Test)

특정 수준의 학교나 교육과정상 적절한 단계에 학습자를 배치시키기 위해 실시된다.

A placement test enables us to sort students into groups according to their language ability at the beginning of a course. Such a test should be as general as possible and should concentrate on testing a wide and representative range of ability in English.

Test Task Specifications	
Category	Description
Purpose	To determine students' current levels and **place them into the most appropriate speaking courses**
Time allocation	2 minutes (1 minute for preparation and 1 minute for speaking)
Task type	Picture-cued tasks
Scoring method	Analytic a. Criteria: Content, Fluency, Accuracy, Pronunciation b. Each criterion is worth 5 points and the score for this task is added up to 20.
Scoring procedure	a. Two examiners: a primary examiner who conducts the test and a secondary examiner who observes the test b. If there is a difference of more than 2 points in total, the examiners discuss rating disagreements based on the recorded test to arrive at a rating that they agree upon.

4 성취도평가(Achievement Test)

성취도평가는 수업, 학습단원, 교육과정이 종료된 후 그 기간 동안 학습한 내용과 목표를 얼마나 숙지하고 달성했는지를 평가한다.

An achievement test is designed to cover a longer period of learning than a progress test. Unlike progress tests, achievement tests should cover as much of the syllabus as possible. They are usually a formal examination, given at the end of the school year or at the end of the course.

5 향상평가(Progress Test)

향상평가는 평가의 실제적 목적 중 가장 중요한 부분이 학생들의 <u>학습이 이뤄지는 언어</u> <u>영역과 능력에서 얼마나 향상되고 있는가</u>를 평가한다.

Perhaps the most important reason is to find out how well the students have mastered the language areas and skills which have just been taught. Unlike most other kinds of tests, progress tests should produce a cluster of high marks. If we test what has recently been taught and practiced, then we should expect students to score fairly high marks. If most of the students fail to score high marks, something must have been wrong with the teaching, the syllabus or the materials. Although you should try to give progress tests regularly, you should avoid over-testing. Moreover, progress tests should be given as informally as possible. The best progress test as a test but see as simply an enjoyable and meaningful activity.

04

Plus ➕

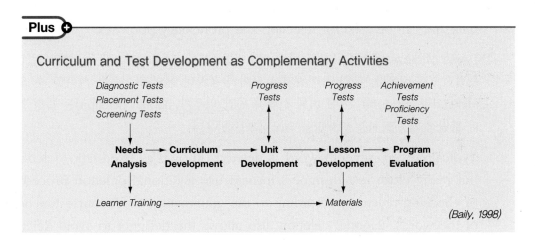

Curriculum and Test Development as Complementary Activities

(Baily, 1998)

04 \ 통합평가와 대안평가

1 Integrative Test

(1) Cloze Test

① **Definition**: 담화를 이룬 텍스트의 일부를 비워놓고 이를 채우게 한다. 빈칸을 채우기 위해서 학습자는 빈칸 앞뒤의 문맥, 어휘, 문장구조, 읽기, 선험지식 등을 활용해야 하므로 대표적인 통합평가에 속한다.

Some teachers do not distinguish between blank-filling and cloze tests, using the term cloze for all blank-filling tests. *In a cloze test, a sentence with a word left out should be filled with a calculated guess, using linguistic expectancies and background knowledge.* Cloze tests are an integrative measure not only of reading ability but also other language abilities. That is, cloze testing is very useful for assessing language proficiency in a short time and can be used for selection and proficiency purposes.

② **Types of cloze tests**: 규칙적 빈칸 비우기(fixed-ratio deletion)는 n번째의 빈칸을 규칙적으로 비운다. 따라서 비워지는 단어의 품사나 문법적 기능은 예측할 수 없다 (deleted in random). 이에 비해 선택적 빈칸 비우기(rational deletion)는 특정 품사나 문법적 기능을 하는 단어만을 의도적으로 비운다.

Typically every seventh word is deleted (known as fixed-ratio deletion), but many cloze test designers instead use a rational deletion procedure of choosing deletions according to the grammatical or discourse functions of the words. Rational deletion also allows the designer to avoid deleting words that would be difficult to predict from the context.

fixed ratio deletion (nth deletion)	주어진 passage의 n번째 어휘를 매번 삭제한다. 작성하기는 쉽지만 n번째에 위치한 단어가 reading comprehension에 중요하지 않거나 문맥상 여러 개의 답이 가능할 수 있다는 단점이 있다.
rational deletion (selective deletion)	특정 학습 요소를 빈칸으로 만드는 방법이다. 예를 들면 관사에 대해 focus를 둔 수업 활동인 경우 관사를 빈칸으로 한다. 신뢰도와 실용성이 높지만 특정 요소만 측정한다는 한계가 있다.

Example ❶

7th Deletion Cloze test

Despite the decrease in size of _____ cultural world, there still remain strong _____ between the usual British and American _____ styles. The question is, how do _____ get your message across? English prose _____ its most novel ideas as if _____ were timeless truths, while American writing _____ if you believe half of what _____ said, that's enough. The former uses _____; the latter, overstatement.

Example ❷

Rational Deletion Cloze Test Focused on Conjunctions

_____ the decrease in size of our cultural world, there still remain strong differences between the usual British _____ American writing styles. The question is, how do you get your message across? English prose conveys its most novel ideas _____ they were timeless truths, _____ American writing exaggerates; _____ you believe half of what is said, that's enough. The former uses understatement; the latter, overstatement.

③ Scoring method of cloze tests

ⓐ **Exact word method**: 원문과 정확히 일치하는 단어에만 점수를 부여하는 채점 방식이다. 채점이 빠르고 신뢰도가 높다.

The students can get credit for a correct answer if and only if the word they write in any give blank is the exact word that was deleted from the original text in that place.

ⓑ **Acceptable word method**: 원문과 같지는 않더라도 문법적이고 문맥에 적합한 단어도 정답으로 인정한다. 신뢰도는 다소 떨어지지만 학생들의 화용론적 능력과 창의성을 키울 수 있다는 장점이 있다.

Any responses that are grammatically correct, and make good sense in the context are given full credit as an acceptable answer. This method may promote positive washback, since it could encourage learners to use their pragmatic expectancy creatively.

(2) C-test

Cloze test의 모호한 채점 기준을 보완하기 위해 사용되는 C-test는 주어진 텍스트의 두 번째 단어마다 빈칸을 두되, 단어의 절반을 제시해 준다. 따라서 정답이 명확하기 때문에 신뢰도가 높다는 장점이 있지만 빈칸 자체에 너무 많은 단서가 주어져서 측정된 읽기 능력에 대한 확실성이 떨어진다는 단점이 있다.

In the C-test, a suggested alternative to the cloze test, the second half of every other word is deleted, leaving the first and the last sentence of the passage intact. Within a C-test, a clue (half the word) serves as a stimulus for respondents to find the other half. It is still not clear to what extent it tests more than microlevel processing. Because half the word is given, students who do not understand the macro-context may still be able to mobilize their vocabulary skills adequately to fill in the appropriate word without engaging in higher-level processing.

Example

Pollution is one of the biggest problems in the world today. Towns a_____ cities a growing, indu_____ is gro_____, and t_____ population o_____ the wo_____ is gro_____. Almost every_____ causes poll_____ in so_____ way o_____ another. T_____ air I_____ filled wi_____ fumes fr_____ factories a_____ vehicles, a_____ there I_____ noise fr_____ airplaned a_____ machines. Riv_____, takes, a_____ seas a_____ polluted b_____ factories and by sewing from our homes.

2) Alternative Test

(1) Characteristics of the Alternative Assessment

① It requires students to perform, create, produce or do something.

② It uses real-world contexts or simulations.

③ It is non-intrusive in that they extend the day-to-day classroom activities.

④ It allows students to be assessed on what they normally do in class every day.

⑤ It uses tasks that represent meaningful instructional activities.

⑥ It focuses on processes as well as products.

⑦ It taps into higher-level thinking and problem-solving skills.

⑧ It provides information about both the strengths and weaknesses of students.

⑨ It is multi-culturally sensitive when properly administered.

⑩ It ensures that people, not machines, do the scoring, using human judgement.

⑪ It encourages open disclosure of standards and rating criteria.

⑫ It calls upon teachers to perform new instructional and assessment roles.

04

Plus ➕

1. Traditional & Alternative Assessment

Traditional Assessment	Alternative Assessment
• One shot, standardized exams	• Continuous long-term assessment
• Timed, multiple-choice format	• Untimed, free-response format
• Decontextualized test items	• Contextualized communicative tasks
• Scores suffice for feedback	• Formative, interactive feedback
• Norm-referenced scores	• Criterion-referenced scores
• Focus on right answer	• Open-ended, creative answer
• Summative	• Formative
• Oriented to product	• Oriented to process
• Foster extrinsic motivation	• Foster intrinsic motivation
• Non-interactive performance	• Interactive performance

2. 수행평가(Performance-based Assessment)

대부분의 대안평가가 수행평가를 기반으로 한다. 즉, 학습자가 직접 수행하는 일련의 과업 과정을 관찰하면서 학습자의 언어능력을 평가한다. 따라서 과업 중심의 평가가 주를 이루며 과제는 실제 생활에서 학습자들이 대면할 수 있는 실제적인 과업을 대상으로 한다.

① It simulates real-life language use.

② It offers open-ended tasks.

③ It allows for creative and divergent responses.

④ It often assesses strategies for constructing a response.

⑤ It requires students to put it all together rather than to recall small pieces of knowledge.

⑥ It promotes recursive rather than linear learning.

⑦ It evaluates performance based on well-defined criteria.

(2) Portfolio

① 개념: 포트폴리오란 학생들의 성취도를 보여주는 결과물을 모아 만든 작품 모음집이다. 포트폴리오는 언어 수행 활동 과정의 결과물을 비교함으로써 자신의 성장 정도를 알 수 있고 학생과 교사의 합의를 통해 스스로 주제를 선택하기 때문에 동기부여에도 도움이 된다.

A portfolio is a collection of student work that tells the viewer about the student. It is important that the student be a participant in the selection of his/her work. In looking over a portfolio, a student, a parent or a teacher will not only see the student in light of her/his language development, but also in terms of his/her cultural background, personality, special abilities, and talents.

Example

Student – teacher Meeting

T : Well, looking back over the last twelve weeks, I can see that you have written many drafts for the three essay writing assignments.

S : Yes, I have. I have a lot of things here.

T : Of all your essays, which one do you think is the best?

S : I think the persuasive essay I wrote is the best.

T : What makes you think so? Maybe you can tell me how you wrote it.

S : Well... I think the topic I chose was quite engaging. I enjoyed the writing process throughout. And it feels good being able to see the progress I've made.

T : Yes, that's the benefit of this kind of project. I can see some improvement in your use of transitions. Your ideas are nicely connected and organized now.

S : Thanks. What else should I include?

T : Well, did you work on the self-assessment form and the editing checklist?

S : Yes, I did. I completed them and included them with all of my drafts right here.

T : Perfect! I'll be able to finish grading all of your work by the end of next week.

T=teacher, S=student

➡ **Portfolios** *can include essays, reports, journals, video or audiorecorded learner language data, students' self-assessment, teachers' written feedback, homework, conference forms, etc.* As collections of these items, **portfolios** can be useful for assessing student performance in that they can lead students to have ownership over their process of learning and allow teachers to pay attention to students' progress as well as achievement.

② **Advantages of portfolios**: 포트폴리오의 가장 큰 장점은 학생들이 자신의 성장 정도를 파악할 수 있다는 것과 자신이 관심 있어 하는 주제를 선택함으로써 동기를 부여하고 자발적인 참여를 유도할 수 있다는 점이다. 또한 학생과 교사 모두에게 학생들의 장점과 약점에 대한 교정적인 정보를 제공하며, 학습자 개인마다 각각의 포트폴리오가 있기 때문에 수준별 학습, 개별화 수업에 적용하기 쉽다.

ⓐ Students are encouraged to use their teachers and classmates as resources.

ⓑ Portfolios are intended to encourage work in which the motivating factor is not that of getting a grade but of becoming more precise writers. Hence, students are encouraged to review and revise their drafts.

ⓒ A portfolio audit by the learner is a good way to stimulate reflective thinking. Students are asked to take stock of what is in their portfolios, what they are still working on.

ⓓ With regard to evaluation of the writing, students can set their own criteria.

ⓔ In the sense of community, the learners and peers share drafts, assist each other while the traditional testing of writing requires solitary work.

ⓕ The portfolios provide teachers with much feedback about their own teaching.

ⓖ It fosters intrinsic motivation, responsibility, and ownership.

ⓗ It promotes student-teacher interaction with the teacher as facilitator.

ⓘ It provides tangible evidence of a student's work.

ⓙ It offers opportunities for collaborative work with peers.

ⓚ It permits assessment of multiple dimensions of language learning.

③ **Guidelines for portfolios**: 포트폴리오는 학생의 자발성을 중시하기 때문에 포트폴리오의 목적을 분명히 함으로써 학생들이 목적에 부여하는 작품을 산출하도록 해야 한다. 또한 open-ended라는 특성으로 인해 채점의 기준이 불분명하기 때문에 채점 기준표를 마련하고 학생들과의 충분한 의사소통을 통해 채점의 신뢰도를 높여야 한다. 마지막으로 교사는 학생들이 포트폴리오가 제공하는 feedback을 충분히 숙지하도록 도움을 줘야 한다.

ⓐ Portfolios can fail if objectives are not clear, if guidelines are not given to students, if systematic periodic review and feedback are not present.

ⓑ Teachers should communicate assessment criteria with students to maintain reliability. The combination of self-assessment and teacher assessment provides students with the maximum benefit.

ⓒ Students are allowed to participate in periodic schedules for review and conferencing. By doing so, they will get valuable feedback and reflect the information about their strength and weakness on the future study.

(3) Journals

① 개념: 학습자가 학습 내용을 포함해 관련된 자신의 생각, 느낌 등을 적은 일지를 총칭한 것을 journal entry라고 하며, 교사와 학생이 교대로 작성할 경우 dialogue journal이 된다.

A journal is a log of one's thoughts, feelings, reactions, assessments, ideas, or progresses toward goals, usually written with little attention to structure, form, or correctness.

② **Advantages of dialogue journals**: Dialogue journal은 학생과 교사의 라포 (rapport)를 형성하고 학생에 대한 정보를 바탕으로 다음 학습 과정을 구성할 수 있도록 하며 사고 과정을 바탕으로 하는 쓰기 능력을 향상시킨다.

ⓐ To carry on a conversation with the teacher

ⓑ To become better equipped to meet students' individual needs

ⓒ To practice in the mechanics of writing, using writing as a thinking process

ⓓ To offer various kinds of feedback

③ Guidelines for dialogue journal

ⓐ Sensitively introduce students to the concept of journal writing and state the objectives of the journal.

학습자들은 dialogue journal이 생소할 수밖에 없다. 따라서 학생들에게 dialogue journal의 개념과 목적을 분명히 알려줘야 한다.

ⓑ Provide optimal feedback in your responses.

학생의 journal에 대한 교사의 feedback은 cheerleading feedback (celebrating success with the students or encouraging them to persevere through difficulties), instructional feedback (suggesting strategies or materials, ways to fine−tune strategy use, or instructing students in their writing), reality−check feedback (helping the students set more realistic expectations for their language abilities)이 있다. 그러나 학생들의 모든 오류에 대한 교정적인 정보보다는 주로 내용적인 측면에서의 응답을 해준다.

ⓒ Provide formative washback comments.

Journal은 학생들의 향상 정도를 알아보는 데 효과적이다. 교사는 학생들에게 문법적인 수정과 점수가 아닌 성장의 정도와 writing에서 나타난 그들의 강점과 약점, 그리고 약점을 보완할 수 있는 comment를 제공하는 것이 바람직하다.

Example

Dialogue Journal Sample

Journal entry by Ming Ling China :

Yesterday at about eight o'clock I was sitting in front of my table holding a fork and eating tasteless noodles which I usually really like to eat but I lost my taste yesterday because I didn't feel well. I had a headache and a fever. My head seemed to be broken. I sometimes felt cold, sometimes hot. I didn't feel comfortable standing up and I didn't feel comfortable sitting down. I hated everything around me. It seemed to me that I got a great pressure from the atmosphere and I could not breath. I was so sleepy since I had taken some medicine which functioned as an antibiotic.

The room was so quiet. I was there by myself and felt very solitary. This dinner reminded me of my mother. Whenever I was sick in China, my mother always took care of me and cooked rice gruel, which has to cook more than three hours and is very delicious, I think. I would be better very soon under the care of my mother. But yesterday, I had to cool by myself even though I was sick, The more I thought, the less I wanted to eat, Half an hour passed. The noodles were cold, but I was still sitting there and thinking about my mother. Finally I threw out the noodles and went to bed.

Teacher's response:

This is a powerful piece of writing because you really communicate what you were feeling. You used vivid details, like "eating tasteless noodles," "my head seemed to be broken" and "rice gruel, which has to cook more than three hours and is very delicious." These make it easy for the reader to picture exactly what you were going through. The other strong point about this piece is that you bring the reader full circle by beginning and ending with "the noodles."

Being alone when you are sick is difficult. Now, I know why you were so quiet in class. If you want to write another entry related to this one, you could have a dialogue with your "sick" self. What would your "healthy" self say to the "sick" self? Is there some advice that could be exchanged about how to prevent illness or how to take care of yourself better when you do get sick? Start the dialogue with your "sick" self speaking first.

(Brown, 2004)

(4) Self-assessment(자가평가)

① 개념: 학습에 있어서 student-centered learning이 중시되면서 학습자 자신에 의한 학습의 평가도 중시되고 있다. 자가평가는 교사나 채점 기준표에 의한 일방적인 평가에서 벗어나 학생 스스로 자신의 학습과 성취물에 대해 평가함으로써 많은 이점을 누릴 수 있다. 자가평가는 형성평가에서 꼭 필요한 평가 방식이며 때로는 자가평가 이외에 peer-assessment와 함께 사용되는데, 주로 checklist를 이용한다.

An important means of continuous assessment takes the form of student self-evaluation. Students are asked to assess themselves each week according to the most appropriate grades listed on a simple form. The students then show their forms at the end of the week and briefly discuss their results individually with a teacher. Whenever possible, teachers can compare their own grades with the grades which students have awarded themselves. Each individual interview will usually take no more than one or two minutes except in rare cases where there is a great discrepancy between a student's self-appraisal and your own view.

Example

A Daily Learning Log

Name: *Jihae Park*

※ Respond to each of the following statements with a checkmark (✔).

	Day 1			Day 2			Day 3			Day 4			Day 5		
	1	2	3	1	2	3	1	2	3	1	2	3	1	2	3
1. I make guesses to understand unfamiliar words.															
2. I first read over passages quickly, and then go back and reread them.															
3. I make summaries of the text that I read in English.															
19. I ask a friend questions about schoolwork.															
20. I write down my feelings in a language learning diary.															

Note: 1 = Never, 2 = Sometimes, 3 = Always

② **Advantages of self-assessment**: 자가평가를 통해 학생들은 학습에 대한 주체 의식, 선택권, 독립성을 키움으로써 학습에서의 autonomy를 높일 수 있다. 또한 자신에 대한 성찰을 통해 만족감을 얻거나 부족함에 대한 전략을 마련함으로써 동기를 부여할 수 있다.

ⓐ It allows students to reevaluate the goals they have set for themselves, to recognize their progress in relation to those goals, and identify new goals revealed as they progress.

ⓑ It heightens their awareness of the goals and outcomes of the program and allows them to identify their strengths and needs in relation to those outcomes.

ⓒ It helps them identify how they learn best; reflect on what they can do as learners.

ⓓ It gives learners a voice in their education and in shaping the curriculum.

③ Guidelines for self-assessment: 학습자들은 self−assessment를 통해 자신의 잠재력을 파악하고 교정적인 정보를 얻을 수 있다. 이러한 긍정적인 효과를 누리기 위해 self−assessment를 지도함에 있어서 주의할 점은 다음과 같다.

ⓐ Tell students the purpose of the assessment.

교사 중심의 수업과 평가에 익숙한 학생들은 자가평가에 혼란스러워할 수도 있다. 자가평가에 대한 학생들의 요구 분석을 바탕으로 자가평가에 대한 올바른 개념과 목적을 알려줘야 한다.

ⓑ Define the tasks clearly.

평가를 하기 전에 학생들이 수행하는 과업에 대한 안내를 명확히 해 목적에 합당한 결과물을 가지고 평가를 하도록 한다. 적절한 자가평가를 위해 교사가 시범을 보일 수도 있으며 checklist 등을 이용할 수 있다.

ⓒ Encourage impartial evaluation of performance or ability.

자가평가의 가장 큰 한계점은 평가에 있어서 주관성이 개입될 가능성이 크다는 점이다. 이를 위해 학생들에게 객관적이고 솔직한 평가가 주는 이점을 보여줄 필요가 있다.

ⓓ Ensure beneficial washback through follow-up tasks.

자가평가가 제공하는 washback 효과를 높이기 위해서 체계적인 follow−up 과정이 필요하다. 교사는 학생들에게 self−analysis의 기회를 주고 학생들의 결과에 대한 comment를 제공해야 한다.

Example ❶

Class Participation

Please fill out this questionnaire by checking the appropriate box.

Yes, Definitely Ⓐ Sometimes Ⓑ Not Yet Ⓒ

a. I come to class on time.   Ⓐ Ⓑ Ⓒ
b. I ask the teacher questions.   Ⓐ Ⓑ Ⓒ
c. I ask my classmates questions.   Ⓐ Ⓑ Ⓒ
d. I answer questions that the teacher asks.   Ⓐ Ⓑ Ⓒ
e. I take equal turns in all three roles.   Ⓐ Ⓑ Ⓒ
f. I cooperate with my group members.   Ⓐ Ⓑ Ⓒ
g. I use the new vocabulary.   Ⓐ Ⓑ Ⓒ
h. I complete all of the peer-reviews.   Ⓐ Ⓑ Ⓒ

comments: _____

Example ②

Learner Log

Circle what you learned and write the page number where you learned it.

a. I can identify buildings.   Yes Maybe No   Page _____
b. I can read maps.   Yes Maybe No   Page _____
c. I can follow directions.   Yes Maybe No   Page _____
d. I can give directions.   Yes Maybe No   Page _____
e. I can use prepositions.   Yes Maybe No   Page _____
f. I can write a letter.   Yes Maybe No   Page _____
g. I can use the simple present and present continuous.
                                                Yes Maybe No   Page _____

Did you answer No to any questions? Review the information with a partner.

Plus ➕

Principled Evaluation of Alternatives to Assessment

	Portfolio	Journal	Self-assessment
Practicality	low	low	mid
Reliability	mid	mid	low
Face Validity	high	mid	mid
Content Validity	high	high	high
Washback	high	high	high
Authenticity	high	high	high

05 \ 채점 방법

1 총괄적 채점 방법(Holistic Scoring Method)

학습자의 과제 수행이나 그 결과를 전체로서 평가해 점수나 레벨 등으로 종합적인 판단을 제공한다. 따라서 피험자의 전체적인 과제 수행 정도를 알아보고자 할 때 적합하다.

(1) 장점

① 채점이 쉽고 시간이 적게 소요된다.
② 언어능력이 수행될 때 세부 능력으로 분리돼 작용하는 것이 아니므로 분석적 방법보다 종합적인 언어능력 채점에 대한 타당도가 높다 (high construct validity).

(2) 단점

① 피험자에 따라서는 특정한 세부 영역이 우수할 수 있지만 이에 대한 고려가 없다.
② 각 하위 영역에 대한 정보를 제공하지 못하므로 진단적인 기능에서는 취약하다 (too weak diagnostic function).

Plus ➕

1. Holistic Rubric

A holistic rubric describes in general terms the qualities of excellent, good, fair, and unsatisfactory assignments. These descriptions can be tied to grades or stand on their own.

Hyunsoo	Description
Grade B (writing)	The 'B' paper shows: • an ability to interpret and develop ideas in the writer's own words • a clear organizational pattern • vocabulary that is adequate in expressing ideas • generally correct use of punctuation or spelling, although with occasional errors • grammar that is usually accurate, and does not interfere with the reader's understanding

2. Primary Trait Scoring

A second method of scoring, primary trait, focuses on "how well students can write within a narrowly defined range of discourse" (Weigle, 2002, p. 110). For example, if the purpose or function of an essay is to persuade the reader to do something, the score for the writing would rise or fall on the accomplishment of that function.

2 분석적 채점 방법(Analytic Scoring Method)

학습자들의 과제 수행을 독립적인 세부(하위) 영역들로 구분해 각각의 점수를 부여한다.

(1) 장점

① 하위 항목에 대한 개별 점수가 교사의 교수 계획에 진단적인 정보를 제공하므로, 학생들의 취약점에 따라 각 영역의 비중을 조절할 수 있다.
② 학생들에게 자신의 강점과 약점에 대한 정보를 제공한다.
③ 하위 영역이 채점자들에게 명료한 기준을 제공하기 때문에 일관성 있고 신뢰성 높은 채점이 가능하다.

(2) 단점

① 언어능력의 종합적인 판단에 대한 정보를 제공하지 못한다.
② 총괄적인 채점 방식에 비해 타당도가 떨어진다.
③ 채점자 훈련과 채점에 시간이 많이 소요된다.

Plus ➕

Analytic Scoring

Classroom evaluation of learning is best served through analytic scoring, in which many as six major elements of writing are scored, thus enabling learners to home in on weaknesses and capitalize on strengths.

Content	30
Organization	20
Vocabulary	20
Syntax	25
Mechanics	5
Total	100

06 선다형 문항

1 선다형 문항(Multiple Choice Items)

(1) 장점

학교 현장에서 많은 교사가 선다형 문항을 선택하는 이유는 주관적이지 않고 <u>객관적으로 평가가 이뤄지며</u>, <u>채점이 용이하고</u>, 특히 true-false items와는 달리 학생들에게 정확한 답에 대한 guessing의 기회를 줄여 주기 때문이다.

Multiple-choice test are fast, easy, and economical to score. They can be scored objectively and thus may give the test the appearance of being fairer and/or more reliable than subjectively scored tests. They reduce the chances of learners guessing the correct answer, in comparison to true-false items.

(2) 단점

Multiple-choice tests는 객관적인 평가이지만 <u>문항 개발에서 주관적 판단이 반영될 수 있으며</u>, 채점은 용이하지만 문항을 작성하기에 매우 까다롭고 노동 집약적이다. 마지막으로 가장 큰 우려는 <u>부정적인 역류효과(negative washback)</u>에 대한 부분이다.

Good multiple choice items are notoriously difficult to write. A great deal of time and effort has to go into their construction. Too many multiple choice tests are written where such care and attention is not given. The result is a set of poor items that cannot possibly provide accurate measurements.

① Multiple-choice tests severely restricts what can be tested.
② It is quite difficult to write successful each item.
③ Washback may be harmful.
④ Cheating may be facilitated.

(3) 구성

모든 multiple-choice item들은 stem(the beginning of the item)과 3, 4, 5개 중 하나의 답안 선택지(answer options, 일반적으로 4개의 선택지를 사용)의 형식을 취하고 있다. 모든 선택지 중 하나만 유일한 정답이며, 나머지 선택지를 흔히 distractor라고 명명한다.

Every multiple-choice items consists of a stem (the beginning of the item) and either three, four, or five answer options (with four options being the most common format). One, and only one, of the options is correct, and that is called disctractors.

2 구성 규칙(Basic Rules of Multiple Choice Items)

(1) Make sure there is <u>only one correct answer</u> for each item.

> **Ex** **Poor test**
>
> I usually go to the dentist to have my teeth _____ once a year.
> ① examined   ② checked   ③ seen   ④ fixed

(2) Make sure the disctractors are <u>the same grammatical class</u> as they key.

> **Ex** **Poor test**
>
> I was hungry, so I went home _____ to eat dinner.
> ① run   ② rate   ③ quickly   ④ rapid

(3) <u>Do not provide inadvertent clues to the key</u> which allow students to answer an item correctly without knowledge of word meanings.

> **Ex** **Poor test**
>
> I want to be poet. I have had an _____ in writing poems, since I was a child.
> ① interest   ② doubt   ③ concern   ④ worry

(4) Make sure <u>the key cannot be selected based on students' world knowledge.</u>

> **Ex** **Poor test**
>
> When tourists from Seoul go to Jeju on vacation, they travel _____.
> ① north   ② west   ③ east   ④ south

Example

A good test which follows ALL guidelines in the above

Inventors are always coming up with new ideas because they are very _____.
① creative   ② sad   ③ lazy   ④ guilty

3 문항 난이도(Item Facility)

문항 난이도는 문제가 얼마나 쉬웠는지, 즉 정답을 맞힐 확률이 어느 정도인지를 나타낸다. *0과 1 사이에서 값이 나오며 1에 가까울수록 정답률이 높고 쉬운 문제이다.*

Item facility(I.F.) is an index of how easy an individual item was for the people who took it. It is a number, typically printed as a decimal, ranging from 0.0 to 1.0. It represents the portion of people who got the item right.

$$\text{I.F.} = \frac{\text{정답자 수}}{\text{전체 학생 수}}$$

(0.0=모두 틀림, 1.0=모두 맞음)

4 오답지 분석(Distractor Analysis)

오답은 정답을 아는 사람과 모르는 사람을 분류하는 기능을 한다. 선다형 테스트를 향상시키기 위해서는 각각의 개별적인 오답이 얼마나 제 기능을 하고 있는지를 아는 것이 중요하다. *너무 많은 학생이 오답을 선택한 경우 그 오답지(distractors)는 학생들의 수준에서 정답을 변별해 내기 어려운 선택지이며, 한 명도 선택하지 않은 오답일 경우 오답으로서의 매력도가 없다고 볼 수 있다.*

Example

Item	A	B	C	D
1	8*	4	0	4
2	4*	3	5	4
3	3	2	0	11*
4	1	8*	2	5
5	5	6	1*	4
6	2	0	2	12*
7	2	10	3*	1
8	1	2	8*	5
9	9*	5	0	2
10	1	8	3	4*
11	7*	4	2	3
12	2	8*	6	0

(*: 정답)

➡ 문항 1의 C, 3의 C, 6의 B, 9의 C, 12의 D는 어느 누구도 선택하지 않았으므로 오답으로서의 제 기능을 수행하지 못했다. 즉, 이 문항들은 4지선다가 아닌 3지선다로서 기능한 셈이므로 선택지의 수정이 필요하다.

➡ 문항 7의 B와 10의 B는 훨씬 많은 학생들이 정답 대신 선택했다. 즉, 이 오답지들은 정답지와 변별하기에는 학생들의 전반적인 수준에서 지나치게 어려운 선택지로서, 역시 수정이 필요하다.

5 문항 변별도(Item Discrimination)

문항 변별도(item discrimination)란 상위 그룹과 하위 그룹을 어느 정도 변별해 내느냐의 정도를 말한다. 변별 지수는 −1~+1 사이의 값을 취한다. 최소한 0.25에서 0.35 이상의 변별도를 지녔을 때 문항 변별도가 있다고 할 수 있다.

$$I.D. = \frac{\text{상위 그룹 정답자 수} - \text{하위 그룹 정답자 수}}{\text{전체 학생 수} \div \text{집단 개수}}$$

+1 = 상위 그룹과 하위 그룹 간의 완벽한 변별
0 = 변별이 없음
−1 = 완벽히 잘못된 변별

Example

Item	High scorers with correct answer	Low scorers with correct answer	I.D.
1	3	1	0.50
2	0	0	0.00
3	4	2	0.50
4	4	1	0.75
5	0	0	0.00
6	4	2	0.50
7	2	1	0.25
8	4	3	0.25
9	3	0	0.75
10	2	0	0.50
11	4	0	1.00
12	2	2	0.00

➡ 문항 2, 5, 12는 학생들의 수준에 무관하게 모두 틀렸거나 모두 맞혔으므로, 상위 그룹과 하위 그룹을 변별하지 못한 문항이므로 반드시 수정이 필요하다.

➡ 문항 11은 상위 수준의 학생들은 모두 맞히고, 하위 수준의 학생들은 모두 틀린 완벽한 변별 지수를 가지고 있는 문항이다.

➡ 문항 7, 8은 가장 낮은 허용 가능한 한계선(I.D.=0.25)에 있으므로 수정을 고려해 봐야 한다.

6] 문항 반응 분포(Item Response Distribution)

문항 반응 분포는 오답지 분석과 변별도 분석을 동시에 나타낸다.

Response frequency distribution combines information from both the distractor analysis and the item discrimination analysis.

Example

		A	B	C	D
item 1	High scorers	3*	0	0	1
	Low scorers	1	2	0	1
item 2	High scorers	0*	0	2	1
	Low scorers	0	2	1	1
item 3	High scorers	0	0	0	4*
	Low scorers	1	1	0	2
⋮			⋮		
item 12	High scorers	0	2*	2	0
	Low scorers	0	2	2	0

(*: 정답)

➡ 문항 1의 경우 상위 그룹과 하위 그룹의 변별을 적절히 해내고 있다. 다만, 선택지 C는 어떤 학생도 선택하지 않은 오답으로서 매력도가 없다.

➡ 문항 2의 경우 상위 그룹과 하위 그룹 모두 정답을 선택하지 않았다. 즉, 학생들의 전반적인 수준에 어려운 문제로 수정이 필요하다.

➡ 문항 3의 경우 상위 그룹과 하위 그룹을 50% 정도 변별해 내고 있다. 다만, 선택지 C는 어떤 학생도 선택하지 않은 오답으로서 매력도가 없다.

➡ 문항 12는 상위 그룹과 하위 그룹이 동일한 수로 정답을 선택했다. 즉, 상위 수준과 하위 수준을 변별하지 못한 문항이다. 또한 선택지 A와 D는 오답으로서 역할을 하지 못해 4지선다가 아닌 2지선다 문항의 역할만 했으므로 수정이 필요하다.

Memo

Build Up

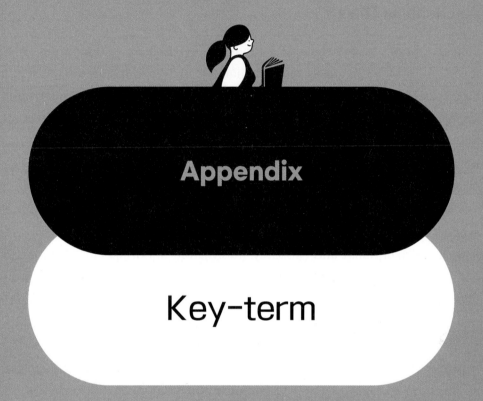

Appendix

Key-term

Key-term

01 \ Schema Theory

Schema theory states that all knowledge is organized into units. Within these units of knowledge, or schemata, is stored information. A schema, then, is a generalized description or a conceptual system for understanding knowledge—how knowledge is represented and how it is used. According to this theory, schemata represent knowledge about concepts: objects and the relationships they have with other objects, situations, events, sequences of events, actions, and sequences of actions.

A simple example is to think of your schema for a dog. Within that schema, you most likely have knowledge about dogs in general (bark, four legs, teeth, hair, tails) and probably information about specific dogs, such as collies (long hair, large, Lassie) or springer spaniels (English, docked tails, liver and white or black and white, Millie). You may also think of dogs within the greater context of animals and other living things; that is, dogs breathe, need food, and reproduce. Your knowledge of dogs might also include the fact that they are mammals and thus are warm-blooded and bear their young as opposed to laying eggs. Depending upon your personal experience, the knowledge of a dog as a pet (domesticated and loyal) or as an animal to fear (likely to bite or attack) may be a part of your schema.

Each new experience incorporates more information into one's schema. What does all this have to do with reading or listening comprehension? Individuals have schemata for everything. Long before students come to school, they develop schemata about everything they experience. Schemata become theories about reality. These theories not only affect the way information is interpreted, thus affecting comprehension, but also continue to change as new information is received.

02 \ Teaching Listening

1 Types of Talks

(1) Transactional Dialogue

Two or more speakers' exchanges to convey propositional or factual information (business type, message-oriented)

(2) Interactional Dialogue

Two or more speakers' exchanges to promote social relationships (social type, person-oriented)

2 Comprehension Process

(1) Bottom-up Processing

A type or cognitive activity that involves learners in the process of recognizing and decoding the individual components of language in order to comprehend a sentence or utterance. Thus, learners start with the basic units of language and combine them to make meaning. Bottom-up processing helps students recognize lexical and pronunciation features to understand the text. Because of their direct focus on language forms at the word and sentence levels, bottom-up exercises are particularly beneficial for lower level students who need to expand their language repertoire. As they become more aware of linguistic features of the input, the speed and accuracy of perceiving and processing aural input will increase. To develop bottom-up processing, students could be asked to...

① Distinguish individual sounds, word boundaries, and stressed syllables
② Listen for intonation patterns in utterances
③ Identify grammatical forms and functions
④ Recognize contractions and connected speech
⑤ Recognize linking words

(2) Top-down Processing

This term refers to a type of cognitive process in which learners draw on their general knowledge and world experiences in order to help them understand the language they encounter. For example, before having learners read a specific text, the teacher may ask them what they know about the topic. Another example is when learners draw on their knowledge of how texts are organized to help them make sense of what they are reading. The other way in which learners might use top-down processing is by recognizing whole words as they are reading, rather than by focusing on each individual letter in order to understand the word. Top-down listening skills include...

① Listening for gist, main ideas, topic, and setting of the text
② Listening for specific information
③ Sequencing the information
④ Predicting
⑤ Guessing
⑥ Inferencing

(3) Interactive Processing

Skilled listeners simultaneously engage in top-down and bottom-up processing, using both types of skills to construct meaning. Although pedagogically people often practice them separately because of their distinctly different focus, they can be addressed within the context of a single listening text.

For example, students are going to listen to a 2-minute-long conversation about getting around the city. Before they begin, they are asked to listen to sentences giving and asking for directions from the conversation and repeat them, paying attention to the intonation, meaning, and grammatical structure of each phrase. They do a fill-in-the-blank exercise, choosing an appropriate form of the verb.

③ Listening Strategies

(1) Predicting

This is for generating the learners' schemata. Pre-listening tasks serve to get the learners to think about and talk about the content of what they are about to hear.

(2) Listening for Global Understanding – Gist

This refers to the general idea of what is being said, as well as who is speaking to whom and why, and how successful they are in communicating their point.

(3) Listening for Specific Information – Scanning

When we don't need to understand everything, but only a very specific part.

(4) Listening for Detail

When we cannot afford to ignore anything because we don't know what kind of information we need.

(5) Inferential Listening

The type of listening we do when we wish to know how the speaker feels. It may involve inferring.

(6) Listening to Confirm Predictions – Monitoring

This is used to confirm predictions made during pre-listening.

4 Extensive vs. Intensive Listening

(1) Extensive Listening (Listening for Pleasure)

All types of listening activities that allow learners to receive a lot of comprehensible and enjoyable listening input. These activities can be teacher-directed dictations or read-alouds or self-directed listening for pleasure that can be done outside the classroom. The key consideration here is that learners get to do a lot of meaningful listening practice.

Extensive listening, (where a teacher encourages students to choose for themselves what they listen to and to do so for pleasure and general language improvement) helps students to improve their listening skills and pronunciation. Extensive listening takes place outside the classroom. Material for extensive listening can be found from several sources; simplified readers with audiotapes, coursebook tapes and tapes of authentic material.

(2) Intensive Listening (Listening for a Purpose)

Use taped material. Most coursebooks include tapes and many teachers rely on them to provide their students; with a good listening course.

Intensive listening is crucial to help students develop effective listening strategies and build bottom-up listening skills, in addition to the top-down skills that are emphasized in global listening activities. Intensive listening may target different goals such as...

① Getting a more detailed understanding of some segments of the text
② Transcribing certain segments in the text
③ Guessing the meaning of a word or phrase from context
④ Looking at certain grammatical structures in the text to see how they can aid comprehension

5 Lesson Procedure

(1) Pre-listening

Pre-listening activities help to focus the learners' minds on the topic, specifying and selecting the items that the students expect to hear, and activating prior knowledge and language structures that have already been met. If the learner knows in advance that they are going to make a certain kind of response, they are immediately provided with a purpose in listening and they know what sort of information to expect and how to react to it. Such activities provide an opportunity to gain some, even if limited, knowledge which will help them to follow the listening text. This knowledge not only provides encouragement but also develops students' confidence in their ability to deal with listening problems.

> ▶ Brainstorming : open-ended, rapid-fire voluntary oral or written listing of ideas with no debate or evaluation by others
>
> Brainstorming is a process for creating a broad list of ideas in response to an initial question or idea. Brainstorming emphasizes broad and creative thinking, inviting all participants' points of view in an effort to ensure that all relevant aspects of an issue or question are considered.
>
> > Ex : If there is a hurricane or another natural disaster, what should we do to be safe?
>
> It's usually a good idea to keep brainstorming focused by using lists and graphic organizers, so students can see the relationship between various ideas.
>
> ▶ Pre-set questions : Presenting comprehension questions before listening to ensure that learners listen with a clear purpose, and that their answers are not dependent on memory.

(2) While-listening

While-listening activities can be shortly defined as all tasks that students are asked to do during the time of listening to the text. The nature of these activities is to help learners to listen for meaning, which is to elicit a message from spoken language. During the while-listening phase, students usually respond somehow to a listening text. They indicate appropriate pictures or answers to multiple-choice questions, complete a cloze test, fill in the blanks of incomplete sentences or a grid, or write short answers to the questions, etc.

(3) Post-listening

The post-listening stage comprises all the exercises which are done after listening to the text. Some of these activities may be the extensions of those carried out at pre- and while-listening work but some may not be related to them at all and present a totally independent part of the listening session. Post-listening activities allow the learners to 'reflect' on the language from the passage; on sound, grammar and vocabulary as they last longer than while-listening activities so the students have time to think, discuss or write.

6 Listening Performance

(1) Dictogloss

A type of classroom activity in which learners take notes while listening to a short L2 passage. Learners are subsequently asked to reconstruct the passage. The primary aim of the activity is for learners to notice gaps in their L2 grammar and vocabulary knowledge as they work on the reconstruction. Often a dictogloss is performed with learners working in pairs or groups, with the goal of having them help each other in reconstructing the passage.

Ex Learners discuss the sea. The teacher then explains the task, and reads a short text on the sea to the class, who just listens. The teacher reads the text again, and the learners take notes. In groups, the learners then reconstruct the text.

In the classroom, Dictogloss is often regarded as multiple skills and systems activity. Learners practice listening, writing and speaking (by working in groups) and use vocabulary, grammar and discourse systems in order to complete the task.

(2) Information Transfer

An information transfer activity involves getting students to put spoken or written texts into another form, such as a chart, grid, picture, table or diagram—or vice-versa. Make sure that the students can't just copy chunks without understanding them by requiring a different organization to the text. These tasks encourage deep processing of information. The interpretation of text, diagram or tables is a skill that is very useful both in academic and everyday life.

> ▶ Advantages of information transfer
> - Information transfer provides a scaffold to assist comprehension. Simply put, the visual support makes listening easier.
> - When used with listening, information transfer focuses on learners' attention on listening without the extra burden of having to read a list of questions or write long answers.
> - These activities encourage deep processing of input, which provides good opportunities to learn new vocabulary and grammatical items contained in the spoken text.

03 \ Teaching Reading

1 Schema Theory

The reader brings information, knowledge, emotion, experience, and culture —that is, schemata—to the printed word. According to Schema theory, reading is only incidentally visual. More information is contributed by the reader than by the print on the page. That is, readers understand what they read because they are able to take the stimulus beyond its graphic representation and assign it membership to an appropriate group of concepts already stored in their memories. Skill in reading depends on the efficient interaction between linguistic knoweldge and knowledge of the world.

(1) Content schemata include what we know about people, the world, culture, and the universe.

(2) Formal schemata consist of our knowledge about language and discourse structure.

> cf In Nassaji's view, background knowledge is not "pre-stored", but "rather it emerges in the context of the task, and is relatively unstructured as opposed to the highly structured knowledge representations suggested by... schema theory."

2 Comprehension Process

(1) Top-down (Concept-driven) Processing

By using the "top-down" processing, readers bring meaning to text based on their experiential background and interpret text based on their prior knowledge.

① The readers sample the text for information and contrast it with their world knowledge, helping to make sense of what is written. The focus here is on the readers as they interact with the text.

② It starts with the hypotheses and predictions then attempts to verify them by working down to the printed stimuli.

(2) Bottom-up (Data-driven) Processing

By using the "bottom-up" processing, the meaning of any text must be "decoded" by the reader and that students are "reading" when they can "sound out" words on a page. (Phonics)

① It uses the ability to decode or put into sound what is seen in a text.

② It starts with the printed stimuli and works its way up to the higher-level stages. The sequence of processing proceeds from the incoming data to higher-level encodings.

(3) Interactive Processing

Reading here is the process of combining textual information with the information the reader brings to a text. The processing involves what is on the written page and what a reader brings to it using both top-down and bottom-up skills. Reading is seen as the interaction between reader and text.

① The overreliance on either mode of processing to the neglect of the other mode has been found to cause reading difficulties for SL learners.

② The interactive processing of reading assumes that skills at all levels are interactively available to process and interpret the text.

③ Good readers are both good decoders and good interpreters of text.

③ Simplified vs. Authentic Texts

(1) Simplified Texts

According to Simensen (1987), simplified texts are texts written ① to illustrate a specific language feature, such as the use of modals or the third-person singular verb form; ② to modify the amount of new lexical input introduced to learners; or ③ to control for propositional input, or a combination thereof.

(2) Authentic Texts

Authentic text may be thought of as any text that was written and published for the public. Journal articles, blog posts and novels are just a few examples. Authentic texts are written for "real world" purposes and audiences: to entertain, inform, explain, guide, document or convince.

4 The Criteria for Choosing Text

(1) Suitability of Content

Among the three main criteria when choosing texts, the suitability of content can be considered to be the most important, in that the reading material should interest the students as well as be relevant to their needs. The texts should motivate as well as.

(2) Exploitability

Exploitability refers to how the text can be used to develop the students' compctcncc as readers. A text that can not be exploited for teaching purposes has no use in the classroom. Just because it is in English does not mean that it can be useful.

(3) Readability

Readability is used to describe the combination of the structural and lexical difficulty of a text, as well as referring to the amount of new vocabulary and any new grammatical forms present. It is important to assess the right level for the right student.

5 Reading Approach

(1) Bottom-up Approach

① **Phonics approach:** It helps students learn letter/sound correspondences so that they can sound out, or "decode," words. Often, they are taught not only basic letter/sound correspondences but rules for pronouncing letters and combinations of letters and for sounding out words. Emphasis on phonics is typically part of "reading readiness" programs.

② **A linguistic approach**: It is based upon the tenets of structural linguists. Those who advocate this particular approach are generally concerned with helping students internalize regular patterns of spelling/sound correspondence, on the assumption that this will enable them to read unfamiliar words without actually stopping to sound them out.

> cf The linguistic approach is like a phonics approach in its emphasis on learning letter/sound patterns, with no specific attention to comprehension. But in another respect, the linguistic approach differs sharply from a phonics approach. Whereas a phonics approach emphasizes the direct teaching of patterns and often conscious learning of rules, the linguistic approach advocates exposing children to regularly spelled words from which children can unconsciously infer common spelling/sound patterns.

③ **A basal approach**: Basal readers are textbooks used to teach reading and associated skills to schoolchildren. Commonly called "reading books" or "readers" they are usually published as anthologies that combine previously published short stories, excerpts of longer narratives, and original works. A standard basal series comes with individual identical books for students, a Teacher's Edition of the book, and a collection of workbooks, assessments, and activities.

(2) Top-down Approach

① **The language experience approach(LEA)**: The Language Experience Approach(LEA) to teaching reading uses the student's own experiences, vocabulary, and language patterns to create texts for reading instruction and make reading a meaningful process.

Students dictate stories to the teacher or orally share a common experience. When written down by or in collaboration with the teacher, these experiences and stories become texts for initial reading instruction.

The stories are accessible because they reflect the language and experience of the learners. This approach is excellent for creating reading texts for beginning-level ESL students whose command of vocabulary and structures in English is limited, as well as for those who are learning to read for the first time.

② **Literature-based approach**: It uses literary selections as major instructional materials that can be tailored to students' interests and needs. In this approach, students can better focus on meaning while reading for their interest and enjoyment.

③ **Whole language approach**: It is a method of teaching students to read by recognizing words as whole pieces of language. Proponents of the whole language philosophy believe that language should not be broken down into letters and combinations of letters and "decoded." Instead, they believe that language is a complete system of making meaning, with words functioning in relation to each other in context.

6 Extensive vs. Intensive Reading

(1) Extensive Reading

For extensive reading, readers spend as much time as possible on reading for pleasure or general language improvement, mostly in real-life situations. Readers choose the text for themselves and tend to read it fast. The materials for extensive reading should be at least 98% comprehensible to the students.

▶ Advantages of extensive reading
- It can provide "massive comprehensible input."
- It can enhance learners' general language competence.
- It can increase knowledge of previously learned vocabulary.
- It can motivate learners to read.
- It teaches learners about the culture of the target language users, which will allow learners to more easily join the L2 speech community.
- It helps to build confidence with extended texts.

---

(2) Intensive Reading

Its goal is to push oneself to build specific skills by taking on difficult material in a focused session.

> ▶ Advantages of intensive reading
> - For low-level readers, intensive reading is possibly the fastest way to build vocabulary. Some foreign language students are able to successfully add 10 or more comprehension words per day.
> - Reading difficult material forces a learner to develop strategies for dealing with texts that are too hard to read comfortably.

7) Reading Strategies

(1) Skimming

Skimming is a high-speed reading technique that can save the reader time and help him/her get through a text quickly. The reader skims to get the general sense of a passage, not specific details. When the reader skims, s/he should not read the whole text and eyes should move very quickly over the lines. The reader should read only the parts of the text that will help him/her answer the questions.

(2) Scanning

Scanning is a very high-speed reading that the reader does when the reader is looking for a specific piece of information. When s/he scans, the reader has a question in mind and does not read every word, only keywords that will answer the question.

(3) Inferencing

The process of putting pieces of information together so that they make sense is called making an inference. In other words, when the reader "infers" something, s/he is drawing an unstated conclusion from the information that s/he already has.

(4) Guessing

When the reader tries to guess the meaning of an unknown word, s/he uses the text surrounding the word—the context—to provide him/her with clues.

(5) Semantic Mapping / Clustering

It is strategy of grouping ideas into meaningful cluster. It helps readers provide some order to a long string of ideas or events from a text. The idea of use this tool is to organize the main ideas of the topic what they are reading. This can be done individually, but it is useful as a productive group work technique as students collectively induce order and hierarchy to a passage.

8 Lesson Procedure

(1) Pre-reading

This stage is intended to construct background knowledge. The teacher becomes a bridge-builder between what students already know about a concept—schemata—and what they need to know in order to understand a particular text, that is, the interaction between those schemata and the input coming from the text.

Pre-reading tasks are intended to prepare the learners for a reading selection, or to give them the first steps in order to develop skills in anticipation and prediction for the reading, activating background knowledge so they could later interact with the text.

(2) While-reading

The aims of this stage are to help students to understand the specific content and to perceive the rhetorical structure of the text. With these tasks, teachers take the learners through the reading and they interact in the text.

(3) Post-reading

This stage is intended to verify and expand the knowledge acquired in the reading. Post-activities are tasks in which learners, after interacting with the reading, reflect, argue and give their points of view. These last tasks also lead the learners to discuss and analyze the issues presented in the reading.

9 Comprehension Level

(1) Literal Comprehension Level

① Involves recognition and recall of ideas and information
② Involves skills reading for facts and central ideas, noting down supporting arguments
③ Literal questions have responses that are directly stated in the text.

(2) Reorganization (or Reinterpretation)

Dealing with the organizing of ideas and information gleaned from various parts of the text

(3) Inferential (Interpretive) Level

① Ideas and information are used as the basis for making intelligent hypotheses.
② Inferential questions have responses that are indirectly stated, implied, or require other information. The reader needs to connect the dots and make conclusions about the material presented in the text to come up with insights that are not explicitly stated in the text.

(4) Evaluative (Critical) Level – Personal Response

① Requires response indicating that an evaluative judgment has been made.
② Evaluative questions require the readers to formulate a response based on their previous reading experience, their life experience, and their opinions on the issues relevant to the text.

(5) Creative (Appreciative) Level

① Involving all the above related dimension of reading, and requiring to be interesting and emotionally, (effectively) sensitive to the ideas and information in the reading selection

② Appreciation includes both the knowledge of, and the emotional response to, literary techniques, forms, styles, and structures.

▶ **The Condition of Text:** Coherence means the connection of ideas at the idea level, and cohesion means the connection of ideas at the sentence level. Basically, coherence refers to the "rhetorical" aspects of your writing, which include developing and supporting your argument (e.g. thesis statement development), synthesizing and integrating readings, organizing and clarifying ideas. The cohesion of writing focuses on the "grammatical" aspects of writing.

▶ **How does the SQ3R method work?**
  - Survey: Scan the main parts of the text you are going to read. This includes looking at the title, headings of paragraphs, introduction and conclusion, first lines of each paragraph, and any extra information that may be presented in boxes on the page. Doing this gives you some basic understanding of what the text is about.
  - Question: If possible, read the questions provided for you FIRST which will help you know what specific information to look for. Questions (those that are provided with text and those provided by your teacher) are designed to focus on the main points. This helps you read with a goal in mind—answering specific questions.

▶ **3R's**
  - Read: Once you have some ideas of what the text is about and what the main points might be, start reading.
  - Recite: If readers do not repeat verbally, they often forget 80%. Writing down the answers to questions from the text and saying these answers will help you remember the information.
  - Review: After you have read and discussed and studied your information, it is important to review your notes again a few days or weeks later.

---

04 \ Teaching Speaking

1 Communicative Competence

The goal of all ESL classes, and particularly work-related classes, according to CLT principle #1 is "communicative competence." Communicative competence involves the ability to converse or correspond with a native speaker of the target language in a real-life situation, with emphasis on communication of ideas rather than simply correctness of language form or knowledge of grammar rules. It is facilitated when learners are engaged in interaction and meaningful communication. Meaningful communication results from students processing content that is relevant, purposeful, interesting and engaging. Communicative competence includes the following:

(1) Grammatical Competence (or Accuracy)

The degree to which the language user has mastered the linguistic code, including vocabulary, grammar, pronunciation, spelling and word formation.

(2) Discourse Competence

The ability to combine ideas to achieve cohesion in form and coherence in thought, above the level of the single sentence

(3) Sociolinguistic Competence

The extent to which utterances can be used or understood appropriately in various social contexts. It includes knowledge of speech acts and functions such as persuading, apologizing and describing.

(4) Strategic Competence

The ability to use strategies like gestures or "talking around" an unknown word in order to overcome limitations in language knowledge; the use of appropriate body (non-verbal) language

2 Characteristics of a Successful Speaking

(1) Produce chunks of language

(2) Produce English stress patterns, words in a stressed and unstressed position, rhythmic structure, and intonational contours

(3) Produce a reduced form of words and phrases

(4) Use an adequate number of lexical units (words) in order to accomplish pragmatic purposes

(5) Produce fluent speech at different rates of delivery

(6) Monitor your own oral production and use various strategic devices—pauses, fillers, self-corrections, backtracking—to enhance the clarity of the message

(7) Use grammatical word classes (noun, verbs, etc.), systems (e.g., tense, agreement, pluralization), word order, patterns, rules, and elliptical forms

(8) Use cohesive devices in spoken discourse

(9) Appropriately accomplish communicative functions according to situations, participants, and goals

(10) Use appropriate registers, implicature, pragmatic conventions, and other sociolinguistic features in face-to-face conversation

(11) Use facial features, kinesics, body language, and other nonverbal cues along with verbal language to convey meanings

3 Principles for Teaching Speaking

(1) Considering Special Language Features in Speaking

① **Connected speech:** Effective speakers of English need to be able not only to produce the individual phoneme of English but also to use fluent connected speech. In connected speech, sounds are modified (assimilation), omitted (elision), added (linking verb), or weakened (through contractions and stress patterning). Due to the complexity of the connected speech, therefore, English teachers should involve the students in activities that are designed to improve their connected speech.

② **Expressive devices:** Some native speakers of English use expressive devices in speaking in some ways, such as changing the pitch and stress of particular parts of utterances, varying volume and speed, and using facial expressions. The use of these devices can contribute to the ability to convey meanings. Therefore, in order to be fully effective communicators, students should be able to employ those devices.

③ **Lexis and grammar:** The use of common lexical and grammatical features can be found in spontaneous speech when performing certain language functions.

④ **Negotiation:** The negotiation is used to seek clarification and to show the structure of the speakers is saying. The speakers need to ask for clarification when listening to someone else. Meanwhile, speakers use negotiated language to show the structure of their thoughts or to reformulate what they are saying in order to be clearer, especially when they know that their talks are not being understood.

(2) Considering the Affective Factor

① **Fear of mistake:** To overcome students' fear of mistakes, emotional bonds between students and teachers should be built. This way, the students are expected to feel comfortable with their teacher and believe that the teacher will help them if they make a mistake. Second, the teacher should improve the students' concentration when learning English. This can be done by creating a supportive learning atmosphere. Finally, the teacher creates a harmonious atmosphere that can reduce students' nervousness.

② **Shyness:** To overcome shyness, Pesce (2011) says that it is urgent that the teacher creates a friendly and open classroom environment. By doing this, shy students are hoped to feel fine of making mistakes in their learning. This way, students will not worry about their imperfect pronunciation and grammar. As a result, they dare to speak in their speaking class.

③ **Anxiety:** In order to overcome anxiety, Koichi Sato (2003) suggests that teachers should be more careful about anxiety which can be intense in students and find techniques that allow students to participate more in oral activities. In addition, providing students with positive reinforcement, motivating students and creating an easy environment in class are important to be noticed by the teacher since it can lower students' anxiety, increase their confidence, and encourage their willingness to communicate. Dealing with anxiety in students' learning, Tsui (in Nunan, 1999) explains that to deal with reluctant students, teachers should accept a variety of answers.

④ **Lack of confidence:** Inhibition or building defenses of one's ego can be manifested as a lack of self-confidence. With regard to a possible solution to overcome the students' lack of confidence, maximizing students' exposure to English is a good way to build the students' confidence. Plus, teachers can provide regular opportunities to practice proper pronunciation and intonation and to converse freely. By doing this, students will experience a greater sense of ability to speak English.

⑤ **High motivation:** To encourage motivation, teachers should provide constant encouragement and support as well as ask questions that reveal the basis of students' problems. Doing this becomes very important because encouragement also gives students a feeling of secure and welcome in their learning. Liu and Huang (2010) say that to overcome students' lack of motivation, teachers can do activities like promoting students' awareness of the importance of English, enhancing students' interest in English, and developing their self-confidence.

4) Accuracy vs. Fluency

There are two main aspects of speaking skill; accuracy and fluency. Accuracy means that the speakers are required to use the correct vocabulary, grammar, and pronunciation. While fluency means that the speakers are required to be able to keep going when speaking spontaneously. However, it does not mean that the speakers speak so fast because sometimes pausing is important. Moreover, when speaking fluently, speakers should be able to get the message across with whatever resources and abilities they have got and regardless of any grammatical and other mistakes. In addition, Harmer (2001b) asserts that the ability to speak fluently is not only knowing the knowledge of language features, but also the ability to process information and language—on the spot.

5) Speaking Stages – PPP vs. TBI Model

(1) PPP Model

① **Presentation**: The instructor starts by introducing a specific language feature (a grammatical structure or a language function) embedded in a context. This is done through providing examples (sentences, dialogues, text excerpts, audio, video, acting out) and using elicitation techniques (e.g., brainstorming, asking questions, use of realia, assigning a controlled pretask).

② **Practice**: The instructor describes a situation (individual, pair, or group work) in which students are to practice the emphasized patterns by reading scripted dialogues or sentences aloud to each other, do completion or matching exercises, ask and answer specified questions, or write examples of the patterns being taught. At this stage, the teacher checks student work for accuracy of form.

③ **Production**: The instructor presents students with an activity in which they are expected to use the forms just practiced. This could be a situation for a role-play, a topic for writing, or any task presumably requiring the use of the language patterns learned.

(2) TBI Model

① **Pre-task**: The introduction to topic and task, through which the teacher prepares the class by exploring the topic, highlighting useful words and phrases, and helping in the understanding of task instructions.

② **Task cycle**: Groups of students do the task proposed under monitoring (Task phrase), plan a report to the whole class on how they did the task and what they found out (Planning phrase), present it, and compare results with other groups (Report phrase).

③ **Language focus**: Students examine and discuss specific features of the material used and the work done in the Task Cycle and the teacher conducts a practice session on new words, phrases, and patterns occurring in the data analyzed.

6 Speaking Activities

(1) Information Gap

In this activity, students are supposed to be working in pairs. One student will have the information that the other partner does not have and the partners will share their information. Information gap activities serve many purposes such as solving a problem or collecting information. Also, each partner plays an important role because the task cannot be completed if the partners do not provide the information the others need. These activities are effective because everybody has the opportunity to talk extensively in the target language.

(2) Jigsaw Activities

A jigsaw task is a specific kind of information gap task, that is, a task that requires learners to communicate with each other in order to fill in missing information and to integrate it with other information.

(3) Role-plays

Students pretend they are in various social contexts and have a variety of social roles. In role-play activities, the teacher gives information to the learners such as who they are and what they think or feel. Thus, the teacher can tell the student that "You are David, you go to the doctor and tell him what happened last night, and…"

(4) Simulations

Simulations are very similar to role-plays but what makes simulations different from role-plays is that they are more elaborate. In simulations, students can bring items to the class to create a realistic environment. For instance, if a student is acting as a singer, she brings a microphone to sing and so on.

(5) Storytelling

Students can briefly summarize a tale or story they heard from somebody beforehand, or they may create their own stories to tell their classmates. Storytelling fosters creative thinking. It also helps students express ideas in the format of beginning, development, and ending, including the characters and setting a story has to have.

(6) Find the difference

Students can work in pairs and each couple is given two different pictures, for example, a picture of boys playing football and another picture of girls playing tennis. Students in pairs discuss the similarities and/or differences in the pictures.

7 Error Treatment

(1) How to Correct Errors

Teachers should be using different strategies and techniques according to the type of error, the learner's personality and the situation; teachers should "make a series of instant judgments about the learner's language ego fragility; anxiety level, confidence, and willingness to accept correction" (Brown, 2007, p. 350). Teachers may, therefore, decide to abandon correction if the error was made by an unconfident, highly anxious learner. It is thus always necessary, as Bartram & Walton (1991) point out, to listen to our students carefully, observe them and evaluate each situation individually.

Teachers should focus on what is right instead of busying themselves over errors. Additionally, teachers should praise students for correct answers, since they will get a feeling of progress in their interlanguage development and become more willing to risk and experiment with language. What teachers must avoid at all costs, on the contrary, is corrective feedback that is derogatory or punitive in any way.

(2) Which Errors to Correct

As Brown (2007) explains, [...] local errors usually need not be corrected since the message is clear and correction might interrupt a learner in the flow of productive communication. Global errors need to be treated in some way since the message may otherwise remain garbled. Global errors, or those that impede intelligibility or interfere with communication, should thus be given priority in the correction. Hendrickson (1978) points out that errors causing the most unfavourable reactions, since they are the most stigmatised should also become high candidates for correction. Besides, errors that occur most frequently should also be seen as needing correction the most. CLT evaluates the seriousness of error from the point of communication: errors that cause a breakdown of communication should be considered the most serious, whereas little details not disturbing easy understanding do not need much treatment.

(3) When to Correct

The basic options regarding timing are either delayed or immediate correction. The problem of immediate correction is that "it often involves interrupting the learner in mid-sentence—a practice which can certainly be disruptive and could eventually inhibit the learner's willingness to speak in class at all" (Allwright & Bailey, 1991, p. 103). In other words, the affective feedback would be negative. On the contrary, psychology literature shows that "feedback becomes less effective as the time between the performance of the skill and the feedback increases" (Allwright & Bailey, 1991, p. 103). This observation makes the decision even more complicated for teachers. Despite all that, teachers have to correct their learners and make decisions regarding the timing of correction on an everyday basis.

(4) Accuracy and Fluency Dichotomy

Immediate feedback is generally preferred by methodologists in activities aimed at accuracy (Ellis, 2009). Accuracy activities are such where students are encouraged to make their utterances as near to a native speaker's as possible—which is usually taken as necessitating more intense correction. Since the aim of such activity is practising newly learned forms and improving one's interlanguage, immediate correction is at place, since it gives the learners instant feedback on how well they are absorbing the new information.

A completely different situation comes with fluency activities, such as roleplaying or free discussions. These are such where learners work on their capacity to communicate within the language. In these activities, methodologists generally dismiss correction at all, since that would mean insisting on accuracy, whereas the aim of such activity is communication and developing student motivation to speak and increasing fluency and ease of expression. Immediate correction might, on the other hand, inhibit students' desire to speak and thus the whole learning process. In order to bring about fluency students need to experience uninterrupted, meaningful communication if they are to learn to use the language.

(5) Ways of Indicating Errors

In explicit correction, the teacher "overtly states that a learner's output was not part of the language-to-be-learned" (Carroll & Swain, 1993; cited in Russell & Spada, 2006, p. 137), whereas in implicit feedback, "learners must infer that the form of their utterance is responsible for the interlocutor's comprehension problems" (Russell & Spada, 2006, p. 137). Lyster & Ranta (1997) defined the above-mentioned types of corrective feedback as follows:

① **Explicit correction:** Providing the correction straight away

② **Recast:** Saying the correct expression without commenting on it or explaining it

③ **Clarification request:** Indicating that the utterance was not understood

④ **Metalinguistic feedback:** Using a technical linguistic explanation of an error

⑤ **Elicitation:** Attempting to elicit the correct form from the speaker

⑥ **Repetition:** Repeating the error, usually with rising intonation or stress

Lyster and Ranta found in their research that recast was the most frequently used type, although it is also the "least likely type of feedback to elicit student repair" (Ellis, 1998, p. 52). As the authors observed, recasts may not be perceived as the correction at all. This is in keeping with an observation by Egi (2007), who found that learners did not sometimes perceive recasts as a type of correction, but rather a reaction to the content. If learners indeed fail to realize they are being corrected, then such a way of indicating error occurrence is seemingly an inadequate one. On the contrary, elicitation and metalinguistic feedback turned out to be the most effective ones, although they dramatically lacked behind recast in the frequency of use (Lyster & Ranta, 1997). All research more or less uniformly shows explicit ways of indicating errors as the more effective ones, with recasts being acceptable with more advanced students.

8 Teaching Conversation

It is important for teachers to be acutely aware of the rules/conventions of conversation and to aid learners to both to perceive those rules and follow them in their own conversations. Without knowledge and use of such rules/conventions, language learners may be reluctant to participate in a conversation because of their inhibitions, or they may be considered obnoxious by their hearers. Brown (2000, p. 255-256) outlines the main processes in conversation:

① Attention getting
② Topic nomination
③ Topic development (including the use of turn-taking and maintaining the conversation through clarification, shifting, avoidance and interruption)
④ Topic termination

These processes may apply to both interpersonal or interactional (social) exchanges and transactional (information) exchanges for goods and services, and conversations may include both types of exchanges.

9 Teaching Pronunciation

(1) Bottom-up Approach

This approach begins with the articulation of individual sounds and works up towards intonation, stress and rhythm. In the bottom-up approach, the basic idea is that if you teach the segments, the suprasegmental features will take care of by themselves.

(2) Top-down Approach

This approach begins with patterns of intonation and brings separate sounds into sharper focus as and when required. In the top-down approach, the assumption is that once the prosodic features are in place, the necessary segmental discriminations will follow accordingly.

(3) **Balanced View** – Focus on Intelligibility (Bottom-up & Top-down)

According to Jenkins (2000), "segmental transfer errors can prove highly detrimental to successful communication in English" (p.39). Along these same lines, and to provide support for her claims, Anderson-Hsieh (2000) reported that "very few studies have actually investigated the relative roles of the segmentals and suprasegmentals in intelligibility, but also that the few that have been conducted have been suggestive (emphasis on original) rather than strongly conclusive of the greater influence of suprasegmentals" (Jenkins, 2000, p. 135).

A satisfactory aim would be to establish a degree of segmental-suprasegmental balance through which learners, for personal or professional reasons, are allowed to choose whether they wish to sound as close as possible to native speakers of English or not. However, even with these needs in place, although it may sound discouraging, many students will never acquire through formal instruction all the suprasegmental features because some of these, especially pitch movement, are plainly not teachable and can only be acquired over time—if at all—through extensive non-pedagogic exposure.

05 \ Teaching Writing

1 Product vs. Process-oriented Approach

(1) Product-oriented Approach

① Focus on "getting it right"
② Controlled tasks following models
③ Final product evaluated

The product-oriented approach to the teaching of writing emphasizes mechanical aspects of writing, such as focusing on grammatical and syntactical structures and imitating models. This approach is primarily concerned with "correctness" and form of the final product.

> ▶ Writing lesson: The writing exercises applied in this approach typically deal with sentence-level writing and paragraph-level organization. Students are often given a framework that illustrates a pattern of rhetorical organization; then, they are asked to fit their ideas into this framework. Both the content and the form which the students deal with are largely controlled by the teacher. Since the main focus of these approaches is on written form, grammar is emphasized and a particular effort is made to avoid errors.

(2) Process-oriented Approach

① Focus on the steps that go into writing
② Giving and receiving feedback and creating multiple drafts
③ Initial focus on ideas/content

The process-oriented approach emphasizes that writing itself is a developmental process that creates self-discovery and meaning. While the mechanical aspects of writing are important, they should not interfere with the composing process. This composing process requires much revision and rewriting. The teacher intervenes and guides students during the composing process but initially does not emphasize "correctness" and the final product;

the emphasis on "correctness" and the final product comes only toward the very end of the writing process. Instead of worrying about form, students concentrate on conveying a written message.

> ▶ Writing lesson: This approach characterizes writing as following a number of processes: first, a writer starts writing ideas as drafts. Subsequently, he checks to see whether the writing and the organization make sense to him or not. After that, he checks whether the writing will be clear to the reader. This approach focuses on how clearly and efficiently a student can express and organize his ideas, not on correctness of form. Students are first asked to go through such writing processes, trying to organize and express their ideas clearly. Students are also taught writing devices used in marking the organization and in making the general coherence clearer.

2 Techniques in Responding to Students' Writing

(1) Correction Symbols

Correction symbols refer to the indication of types and locations of students' mistakes through the use of correction codes. The application of correction codes is normally done by underlining the mistakes and using some kind of symbols to focus the attention of the students on the kind of mistake they have made. So, the coding technique consists of using a number of different codes to refer to the different aspects of language such as word order, spelling, verb, tense, etc. Correction symbols are also called minimal marking. Using correction codes is a convenient way of giving learners information on where they have gone wrong and it is convenient to have a system of signals to the pupil in order to help him to know what he is looking for before he has acquired much proof-reading skill. In addition, this technique makes corrections neater and less threatening than masses of red ink and helps students to find and identify their mistakes.

• Correction Codes •

→	Indent this line
?	I'm not sure what you mean
I	Divide letters or words
SC	Sentence combining error (fragment or run-on)
^	Add something here
a̲ A̲	Change to capital or lowercase
¶	Begin a new paragraph here
WO	Word order
SP	Spelling error
P	Punctuation/capitalization
VT	Verb tense
WC	Word choice
WF	Word form
□	Take out the space

(2) Conferencing

Teachers should meet with individual students to comment and give advice on assignments. Such meetings are called conferencing. Conferencing provides a student with a chance to discuss the strengths and weaknesses of his writing with the teacher. Teachers should remind students that academic progress rests on the student's shoulders and not the teacher's. When teachers are going over writing errors, they can prompt students for the corrections with hints or general error identification rather than provide the actual corrections themselves. During conferencing, the other students in the class can be assigned exercises or work on their assignments while the teacher meets with each individual.

(3) Writing Comments

Teachers can provide comments on content and organization to improve students' writings.

Ex❶ "This is a good first try, but your topic sentence should be more specific and unique."

Ex❷ "Nice job moving from argument to example!"

Ex❸ "This is a nice paragraph. But I think you could improve it by giving me more details about the rich man and his son. Why, exactly, did he not allow his son to go to school."

(4) Checklist

The teacher can make a checklist that asks editors to check for the various areas in a piece of writing. The checklist may ask editors, "Does the introduction contain a hook?," "Does the paper have a well-defined thesis?," "Do all the paragraphs have strong supporting sentences?," and so forth. It's best that teachers model an example of how to use the checklist with an example well-written passage and a poorly-written one and respond to them with a copy of a checklist for each on an overhead projector for comparison. By seeing the detail you put in the responses to each checklist, students will have an idea of what is expected of them as editors to their classmate's writing.

(5) Peer-editing

Editing a peer's piece of writing is called peer-editing. Some students may see peer-editing as unbeneficial to learning and may prefer teachers to do all the editing. Peer-editing allows students to identify each other's strengths and weaknesses in their writing skills while being less reliant on the teacher. When students experience peer-editing, they become more empowered, and more objective in their writing.

3 Writing Activities (Controlled to Free Writing)

(1) Controlled (Intensive) Writing

Controlled writing, also known as guided writing, has been a tradition for a long time in English as second/foreign language classrooms. It is still considered an effective tool in helping learners put words down on paper. Unlike freewriting, controlled writing takes place when learners are supplied with "a great deal of the content and/or form [such as] an outline to complete, a paragraph to manipulate, a model to follow, or a passage to continue." Controlled writing assists in both preventing errors that apparently occur from first language interference and reinforcing proper use of second language patterns. Therefore, engaging learners in controlled writing in L2 can be "as an exercise in habit formation (in which the ESL/EFL learner) is simply a manipulator of previously learned language structures."

> ▶ Dicto-composition: A paragraph is read at normal speed, usually two or three times; then the teacher asks students to re-write the paragraph to the best of their recollection of the reading. In one of several variations of the dicto-comp techniques, the teacher, after reading the passage, puts key words from the paragraph, in sequence, on the chalkboard as cues for the students.
>
> ▶ Sentence combining: Combining sentences encourages a writer to take two or more short, choppy sentences and combine them into one effective sentence. By learning this skill, students enhance their writing style. Sentence combining skill is something that will develop over several short practice sessions and should be considered as one component of an overall writing program.

(2) Freewriting

The Freewriting Approach is essentially based on the belief that when we write freely and frequently, we improve our ability in that language skill. Freewriting means that the students write without teacher's interference, and are encouraged to emphasize content and fluency first. Once the ideas are expressed on paper, the teacher intervenes to provide some assistance to improve grammatical accuracy.

Learners write for a period of time in class on a topic of interest to them. This writing can take many forms, including quick writings, which are time-limited, done individually, and not always shared; and dialogue journals, written to a teacher, a classmate or another partner who then responds.

> ▶ Dialogue journals: Dialogue journals are written conversations in which a learner and teacher (or another writing partner) communicate regularly (daily, weekly, or on a schedule that fits the educational setting) over a semester, school year, or course. Learners write as much as they choose on a wide range of topics and in a variety of genres and styles. The teacher writes back regularly, responding to questions and comments, introducing new topics, or asking questions. The teacher is primarily a participant in an ongoing, written conversation with the learner rather than an evaluator who corrects or comments on the quality of the learner's writing. Topics for or types of writing may be specified to enhance the curriculum, and some correction may be given by the teacher, but the primary goal of the writing is communication.

(3) Genre Writing

The genre approach to teaching writing is mainly concerned, as the name indicates, on teaching particular genres that students need control of in order to succeed in particular situations. This might include an emphasis on the content of the text as well as the context in which the text is produced. The fundamental principle that underlies the genre-based approach is that language is functional; that is, it is through language that we achieve certain goals. Another important aspect of this view is the one that sees language as occurring in particular cultural and social contexts, and thus, cannot be understood outside its context. Particular genres are used to fulfill particular social functions in particular contexts. Language, then, is not to be separated from the social and cultural context in which it appears. The objective of adopting the genre approach is to enable students to use appropriate registers which are important for them.

4 Principles for Teaching Writing Skills

(1) Incorporate practices of "Good" writers

① Focus on a goal or main idea

② Spend some time planning to write

③ Easily let your first ideas flow onto the paper

④ Follow a general organizational plan as you write

⑤ Solicit and utilize feedback on your writing

⑥ Revise your work willingly and efficiently

⑦ Patiently make as many revisions as needed

(2) Balance process and product

(3) Account for cultural/literary background

If there are some apparent contrasts between students' native traditions (rhetorical conventions) and those that you are trying to teach, try to help your students to understand what it is exactly and make them use acceptable English rhetoric.

(4) Connect reading and writing

Students learn to write in part by carefully observing what is already written. That is, they learn by observing, or reading, the written word.

(5) Provide as much authentic writing as possible

Sharing writing with other students in the class is one way to add authenticity. Publishing a class newsletter, writing letters to people outside of class, writing a script for a skit or dramatic presentation, writing a resume, writing advertisements—all these can be seen as authentic writing.

(6) Design prewriting, drafting, and revising stages of writing

① Prewriting stage encourages the generation of ideas. One technique is brainstorming. It allows students to get their "creative juices flowing." In the first draft stage, freewriting, like brainstorming, is a useful way for students to simply start the "flow" of writing, unfettered by the potential of being judged for ungrammaticalities, incorrect spelling, or fuzzy thinking.

② The drafting and revising stages are the core of process writing. Drafting is viewed as an important and complex set of strategies, the mastery of which takes time, patience, and trained instruction.

③ Evaluation of the final written product, especially peer-and self-assessment, could be a complex process for students. If that's the case, it should be made clear that the purpose of such an evaluation is to be formative in suggesting ways to improve their writings the next time around.

(7) Strive to offer techniques that are as interactive as possible

It is clear that process-oriented approach to writing instruction is interactive as students work in pairs and groups to generate ideas and to peer-edit as well as learner-centered with ample opportunities for students to initiate activity and exchange ideas. Writing techniques that focus on purposes such as letters, forms, memos, directions, and short reports are also subject to the principles of interactive classrooms.

(8) Be a facilitator, not a judge, in responding to students' writing

When you respond to an error, remember to allow students to notice their errors and then to self-correct.

① Responding to a first draft

ⓐ Resist the temptation to treat minor (local) grammatical errors.

ⓑ Major (global) errors may be indicated either directly by underlining or indirectly by a check next to the line in which an error occurs.

ⓒ Comment holistically, in terms of the clarity of the overall thesis, main idea, and the general structural organization.

② Commenting on second and third drafts

ⓐ Minor (local) grammatical and mechanical (spelling, punctuation) errors should be indicated, but not corrected by the teacher.

ⓑ Comment on the specific clarity and strength of main ideas, supporting ideas and on argument and logic.

ⓒ Comment on word choices and expressions that may not be as clear or direct as they could be.

ⓓ Check cohesive devices within and across paragraphs.

(9) Explain rhetorical, formal conventions of writing

Each genre of writing has its formal properties. Don't just assume that students will pick these up by absorption. Make them explicit. A reading approach to writing is very helpful here.

06 \ Teaching Vocabulary

1 Intentional vs Incidental Learning

(1) Intentional (Explicit) Learning

Learning that occurs with awareness of the L2 feature that is being learned and with an intention to learn that feature. Explicit learning often results in explicit knowledge; however, it is arguably possible for explicit learning to contribute to implicit knowledge.

Explicit instruction involves diagnosing the words learners need to know, presenting words for the first time, elaborating word knowledge, and developing fluency with known words. Some guidelines for explicit instruction are as follows:

① Diagnose which of the 3,000 most common words learners need to study

② Provide opportunities for the intentional learning of vocabulary, elaborating word knowledge, and developing fluency with known vocabulary

(2) Incidental Learning

Learning that happens without the learner intending for it to occur. For example, learners may be involved in a communicative activity in which they are discussing a specific topic. Thus, primary intention is for them to practise speaking the L2. However, during that activity, a learner may notice and learn a specific lexical item or grammatical structure. Incidental learning can also occur when learners are focused on learning targeted grammatical structures (intentional learning), but become aware of the other linguistic items that are not specifically the target of instruction at the moment. One are in which incidental learning has been a focus of investigation is vocabulary. In particular, research has investigated the role of extensive reading on learners' incidental learning of vocabulary.

Graded learners are to build up their vocabulary and structure until they can graduate to more authentic materials. Low-proficiency learners can benefit from graded readers because they will be repeatedly exposed to high-frequency vocabulary.

It may be initially useful to devote some class time to Sustained Silent Reading (SSR) for many students who may never have done extensive reading for pleasure. Once students develop the ability to read in a sustained fashion then most of the reading should be done outside of class.

2 Frequency

Various researchers have asserted that learners should receive explicit instruction and practice for the first two to three thousand high-frequency words and beyond this threshold level, most low frequency words will be learned implicitly while reading or listening. The reason is that it is very difficult to guess the meaning of new words unless many words on a page are known. According to Nation (2003), being familiar with the high-frequency words is the "essential basis of all language use and deserves a great deal of attention in language teaching materials."

3 Guessing Meaning from the Context

Guessing from context is a case in point. Hunt and Beglar (2002) believe that learners need to know about 19 out of 20 words in order to guess successfully from context. Kelly (1990) asserts that since guessing from context fails to direct attention to word form and meaning, relatively little learning occurs. However, Hunt and Beglar add, "Although this strategy often may not result in gaining a full understanding of word meaning and form, guessing from context may still contribute to vocabulary learning" (p. 262). Furthermore, more proficient learners use this strategy more effectively than low proficiency ones. Nation and Coady's (1988) five-step procedures are for guessing as follows:

(1) Determine the part of speech of the unknown word

(2) Look at the immediate context and simplify it if necessary

(3) Look at the wider context. This entails examining the clause with the unknown word and its relationship to the surrounding clauses and sentences

(4) Guess the meaning of the unknown word

(5) Check that the guess is correct

4 Vocabulary Analysis

(1) Look for prefixes (co–, inter–, un–, etc.) that may give a clue

(2) Look for suffixes (–tion, –tive, –ally, etc.) that may indicate what part of speech it is

(3) Look for roots that are familiar (e.g. 'intervening' may be a word that a student doesn't know, but recognizing that the root 'ven' comes from Latin 'to come' would yield the meaning 'to come in between')

5 Techniques

(1) Keyword Strategy

The keyword method is mnemonic. The keyword method, a valuable technique used to memorize the meaning behind vocabulary words, is when a person uses what a word sounds like to visualize something memorable that will help them later recall the definition.

Let's look at the word, 'aplomb.' This is a common middle-school vocabulary word. It means, 'coolness and composure under strain.' When the fantasy character Harry Potter faced the villain, he remained aplomb although he knew he was about to die. A student studying this vocabulary word could say that 'aplomb' sounds a bit like 'a plum' and they could visualize a cold plum straight from the refrigerator that remained cool and composed even though it was underneath a lot of other fruits and vegetables ('under strain'). When it comes time for their vocabulary test, the word 'aplomb' will carry with it this visualization, which will trigger the definition.

(2) Word Map

A word map is a strategy to help learners learn new vocabulary words. There are many different variations on how to use this strategy. One way is to use the four-corner vocabulary chart, and with this method, students write the definition, use it in a sentence, draw a picture of the word, and write the word in the corner.

Other methods to use this strategy are to add antonyms, synonyms, dictionary definitions, part of speech and more. This strategy can be adjusted to meet the needs of all learners. Throughout this strategy students are making personal connections, because they are drawing their own picture, writing their own sentences and the definition in their own words. By doing this, it gives more meaning to learning the vocabulary word, and this would help struggling readers tremendously. Graphic organizers are helpful for all learners because it really helps them organize their thoughts. According to Echevarria, Vogt & Short (2014), "These charts provide more context and "clues" than typical word walls because they include an illustration, definition, and sentence for each vocabulary word."

(3) Concordancer

A concordancer is a computer program that automatically constructs a concordance. The output of a concordancer may serve as input to a translation memory system for computer-assisted translation, or as an early step in machine translation. Concordancers are also used in corpus linguistics to retrieve alphabetically or otherwise sorted lists of linguistic data from the corpus in question, which the corpus linguist then analyzes. A number of concordancers have been published notably Oxford Concordance Program, a concordancer first released in 1981 by Oxford University Computing Services claims to be used in over 200 organisations worldwide.

07 \ Teaching Grammar

1) Approach to FFI (Form–focused Instruction)

By the advent of communicative language teaching, there was a shift to meaning-based approaches in which meaning was focused at the expense of form. However, this purely meaning-based approach may deprive language learners of the acquisition of target morpho-syntactic forms or features. Striking a balance between meaning and forms-focused instruction enticed the researchers to come up with the focus-on-form approach which facilitates interlanguage restructuring through form-function mapping.

(1) Focus on Meaning

Focus on meaning does not allow for any attention whatsoever to the linguistic code of the L2. The assumption behind this approach is that an L2 is learned best by allowing students to experience the L2 through communication and not through rigorous study (e.g., Krashen's Natural Approach, immersion programs).

(2) Focus on Forms

Focus on forms involves more traditional approaches to grammar that consist of isolating individual linguistic constructs out of context. Long and Crookes (1992) define focus on forms as "the use of some kind of synthetic syllabus and/or a linguistically isolating teaching method, such as audiolingualism, the Silent Way, or Total Physical Response. Long and Crookes (1993) go on to point out that a focus on forms involves "treatment of a language as an object, as the content of the syllabus and primary focus of instruction" whereas focus on form involves "treatment of language as an object in context as an incidental feature of task accomplishment."

(3) Focus on Form

"An occasional shift of attention to linguistic code features by the teacher and/ or one or more students triggered by perceived problems with comprehension or production." Long (1991) asserts that focus on form is when the instructor intentionally draws attention to linguistic elements of the L2 but maintains an overriding focus on meaning and communication.

2 Deductive vs. Inductive Approach

(1) Deductive Approach

A deductive approach involves the learners being given a general rule, which is then applied to specific language examples and honed through practice exercises.

(2) Inductive Approach

An inductive approach involves the learners detecting, or noticing, patterns and working out a 'rule' for themselves before they practise the language.

(3) Abductive Approach

An abductive approach involves the learners understanding hidden rules of language use through the process of exploring hypotheses and inferences.

A teacher can start with abduction, taking experiential and exploratory approaches (e.g., puzzle-based learning) and then move on to either inductive or deductive tasks as relevant, followed with future exploration at a wider or deeper level.

▶ Which approach – pros and cons?

- First and foremost, it is perhaps the nature of the language being taught that determines if an inductive approach is possible. Inductive learning is an option for language with salient features and consistency and simplicity of use and form. The basic forms of comparative adjectives (*easier than, more intelligent than, busier than, less interesting than*) is an example of this. Conversely, teaching the finer points of the use of articles (a/an, the) inductively, for example, would most probably be problematic.

- The learner-centered nature of inductive teaching is often seen as advantageous as the learner is more active in the learning process rather than being a passive recipient. This increased engagement may help the learner to ① develop a deeper understanding and help fix the language being learned. This could also ② promote the strategy of 'noticing' in the student and enhance learner autonomy and motivation.

- Inductive learning can be more time- and energy-consuming and more demanding of the teacher and the learner. It is also possible that during the process, the learner may arrive at an incorrect inference or produce an incorrect or incomplete rule. Also, an inductive approach may frustrate learners whose personal learning style and/or past learning experience is more in line with being taught via a more teacher-centred and deductive approach.

- While it might be appropriate at times to articulate a rule and then proceed to instances, most of the evidence in communicative second language teaching points to the superiority of an inductive approach to rules and generalizations.

3 Explicit (knowing the rule) vs. Implicit (pick up a language) Grammar Instruction

Explicit instruction refers to instruction that incorporates the presentation and explanation of language rules and/or directions to attend to particular language structures. If neither one of these two conditions is present, the treatment of grammar is regarded as implicit.

(1) Pros of Explicit Grammar Instruction

① **Learning a language**: Explicit grammar instruction is conducive for "knowing the rules" of a language. In addition, it provides a solid knowledge of grammar and syntax. In other words, this all amounts to mastering how the language works.

② **Reveals exceptions**: Explicit grammar instruction is useful for pointing out the particularities of a language, the exceptions. For example, overtly discussing word order and irregular verbs in the English language results in a greater awareness of the intricacies of the language.

③ **Better for some, but not all**: It seems to be the case that some people are just better explicit learners. Logical, mathematical and verbal types of intelligence seem to be more readily inclined to learn and adopt grammar explicitly.

④ **Better for adult learners**: Our capacity to acquire new languages declines as we age. As a result, this also means that explicit grammar instruction becomes more relevant as we get older as well. "Formal" language learning seems to be a better approach for adult learners.

(2) Pros of Implicit Grammar Instruction (= Cons of Explicit Grammar Instruction)

① **Acquiring a language**: Implicit grammar instruction is better for "picking up a language" or arriving at the practical use of a foreign language. Implicit instruction therefore helps the learner prepare for natural, communicative situations where rules are often forgotten or broken.

② **Achieving fluency**: Implicit grammar instruction is actually the way we acquire our very first language at an early age. When we are little we do not pay attention to the rules behind language but rather how it works in practical, real situations. Implicit instruction, therefore, promotes the gaining of basic linguistic skills that are essential to language.

③ **Promoting actual memorization**: Probably the greatest threat of explicit grammar instruction is the danger of empty memorization. By promoting the "knowledge of rules," explicit instruction also encourages a superficial acquisition of the language. Without knowing how to apply them, rules are pretty much useless.

4 Declarative vs. Procedural Knowledge

Language teachers and language learners are often frustrated by the disconnect between knowing the rules of grammar and being able to apply those rules automatically in listening, speaking, reading, and writing. This disconnect reflects a separation between declarative knowledge and procedural knowledge.

(1) Declarative Knowledge

Declarative knowledge is knowledge about something. Declarative knowledge enables a student to describe a rule of grammar and apply it in pattern practice drills.

(2) Procedural Knowledge

Procedural knowledge is knowledge of how to do something. Procedural knowledge enables a student to apply a rule of grammar in communication.

Procedural knowledge does not translate automatically into declarative knowledge. Many native speakers can use their language clearly and correctly without being able to state the rules of its grammar. Likewise, declarative knowledge does not translate automatically into procedural knowledge. Students may be able to state a grammar rule, but consistently fail to apply the rule when speaking or writing.

⟨ 5 ⟩ Grammar Techniques

(1) Input Enhancement

Input enhancement is a focus on form task in which specific target structures are highlighted for the purpose of implicit instruction. Sharwood-Smith (1981) argues that internalization of the target forms, as well as meaning, occurs through improving the quality of input via typical input enhancement techniques such as *color-coding, boldfacing, underlining, italicizing, capitalizing, and highlighting* for textual enhancement purposes and oral repetition for aural enhancement purpose.

It is claimed that this technique brings the forms into focal attention, and according to Schmidt (2001), some L2 components are so subtle and abstract that they cannot be attended to; therefore, one of the important functions of language teaching is to help focus learners' attention on the linguistic aspects.

(2) Input Flooding

Flooding learners with specific forms of the target language in order to draw learners' attention to the input. It presents texts that contain a target structure that appears frequently or repeatedly, and is therefore more salient. This may trigger syntactic priming, as speakers tend to "produce a previously spoken or heard structure."

(3) Input Processing

Input processing tries to provide an elaboration on how learners achieve 'form' from the input and how they parse sentences during the act of comprehension while their focal attention is on meaning. The overall aim of input processing tasks is to improve learners' intake which is not all input learners are exposed to, but the input learners actually comprehend in terms of form, function, and meaning. It is important that the text used for input remain reasonably natural, and that the learners make the necessary connections between form and function in authentic contexts of L2 use.

(4) Dictogloss

A variation on the *dictocomp* technique. It is a task-based procedure designed to help L2 learners internalize certain grammatical elements that are built into a text. Through the reconstruction of a text, students come to notice certain grammatical features. Before the reconstruction stage, students are not asked to notice a grammatical form, even though they are embedded in the text. Only at the last stage of the procedure will students possibly become aware of using the form.

(5) Consciousness-raising Tasks

Ellis et al. (2001) define consciousness-raising tasks as a pedagogic activity where the learners are provided with second language data in some form and required to perform some operation on it, the purpose of which is to arrive at an explicit understanding of the target grammar. The consciousness-raising tasks seem to be similar to the PPP (presentation, practice, production) model, but one significant difference is clear. In the PPP model, students are required to use a target form in speaking or writing. However, in consciousness-raising tasks what learners should be able to do is not to use the form in speaking and writing but to find the rule and understand the target form in terms of form, meaning, and function.

(6) Garden Path

In the garden path, which is the most explicit technique, a teacher takes learners into making overgeneralization regarding a grammatical rule so that the learners can notice the form more impressively. That is, when a teacher plans to teach a certain target form, the teacher only briefly explains the major rules of the form instead of its exceptions. Then, the teacher corrects students' errors, providing the rule of the exceptions when students' overgeneralization actually occur.

08 \ Principles of Language Assessment

1 Practicality

An effective test is practical. A prohibitively expensive test is impractical. A test of language proficiency that takes a student five hours to complete is impractical—it consumes more time (and money) than necessary to accomplish its objective. A test that requires individual one-on-one proctoring is impractical for a group of several hundred test-takers and only a handful of examiners. A test that takes a few minutes for a student to take and several hours for an examiner to evaluate is impractical for most classroom situations. A test that can be scored only by computer is impractical if the test takes place a thousand miles away from the nearest computer. The value and quality of a test sometimes hinge on such nitty-gritty, practical considerations.

2 Reliability

A reliable test is consistent and dependable. If you give the same test to the same student or matched students on two different occasions, the test should yield similar results.

(1) Student-related Reliability

The most common learner-related issue in reliability is caused by temporary illness, fatigue, a "bad day," anxiety, and other physical or psychological factors, which may make an "observed" score deviate from one's "true" score. Also included in this category are such factors as a test-taker's "test-wiseness" or strategies for efficient test-taking.

(2) Intra-rater Reliability

The degree of agreement among repeated administrations of a diagnostic test performed by a single rater.

(3) Inter-rater Reliability

Human error, subjectivity, and bias may enter into the scoring process. Inter-rater reliability occurs when two or more scorers yield inconsistent scores of the same test, possibly for lack of attention to scoring criteria, inexperience, inattention, or even preconceived biases. In the story above about the placement test, the initial scoring plan for the dictations was found to be unreliable—that is, the two scorers were not applying the same standards.

3 Validity

The extent to which inferences made from assessment results are appropriate, meaningful, and useful in terms of the purpose of the assessment.

(1) Construct Validity

A construct is any theory, hypothesis, or model that attempts to explain observed phenomena in our universe of perceptions. "Proficiency" and "communicative competence" are a linguistic construct. Construct validity asks, "Does this test actually tap into the theoretical construct as it has been defined?"

(2) Content Validity

If a test actually samples the subject matter about which conclusions are to be drawn, and if it requires the test-taker to perform the behavior that is being measured, it can claim content-related evidence of validity, often popularly referred to as content validity.

(3) Criterion Validity

The extent to which the "criterion" of the test has actually been reached. In the case of teacher-made classroom assessments, criterion-related evidence is best demonstrated through a comparison of results of an assessment with results of some other measure of the same criterion.

① **Concurrent validity**： A test has concurrent validity if its results are supported by other concurrent performance.

② **Predictive validity**： The predictive validity of an assessment becomes important in the case of placement tests, admissions assessment batteries, language aptitude tests, and the like. The assessment criterion in such cases is not to measure concurrent ability but to assess (and predict) a test-taker's likelihood of future success.

(4) Face Validity

The extent to which students view the assessment as fair, relevant, and useful for improving learning. Face validity means that students perceive the test to be valid. It will be perceived valid if it samples the actual content of what learners has achieved or expect to achieve.

4 Authenticity

The degree of correspondence of the characteristics of a given language test task to the features of a target language task. Essentially, when you make a claim for authenticity in a test task, you are saying that this task is likely to be enacted in the "real world."

5 Washback

The effects, both beneficial and detrimental, of an assessment on teaching and learning prior to and after the assessment itself. When students take a test, ideally they will receive feedback about their competence, based on their performance. The feedback should "wash back" to them in the form of useful diagnoses of strengths and weaknesses. In the case of informal assessment, it is more likely to have built-in washback effects by nature, because the teacher usually provides interactive feedback. A formal test also can have positive washback, but it is also subject to an absence of washback if students simply receive a letter grade or a single overall numberical score.

09 \ Types of Assessment

1 Formative vs. Summative Test

(1) Formative Test (Assessment for Learning)

Formative assessment is used to aid learning. In an educational setting, formative assessment might be a teacher (or peer) or the learner providing feedback on a student's work, and would not necessarily be used for grading purposes. Formative assessments are diagnostic.

(2) Summative Test (Assessment of Learning)

Summative assessment is generally carried out at the end of a course or project. In an educational setting, summative assessments are typically used to assign students a course grade. These types of assessments are generally evaluative.

2 Direct vs. Indirect Test

(1) Direct Test

Direct testing involves the test-taker in actually performing the target task.

(2) Indirect Test

In an indirect test, learners are not performing the task itself but rather a task that is related in some way.

3 Objective vs. Subjective Test

(1) Objective Test (e.g., multiple-choice, true or false answers, matching questions)

Objective assessment is a form of questioning that has a single correct answer.

(2) Subjective Test (e.g., extended-response questions, essays)

Subjective assessment is a form of questioning that may have more than one correct answer (or more than one way of expressing the correct answer).

4) Referencing

(1) Criterion-referenced Assessment

Criterion-referenced assessment occurs when candidates are measured against defined (and objective) criteria. The best known example of a criterion-referenced assessment is the driving test. Learner drivers are measured against a range of explicit criteria (such as "not endangering other road users").

• Speaking Rubric •

	Level 1	Level 2	Level 3	Level 4
Reasoning (makes sense)	The student reasons inconsistently and with limited understanding.	The student reasons consistently and with limited understanding.	The student reasons consistently and with general understanding.	The student reasons consistently and with thorough understanding. The student uses complex ideas.
Communication (vocabulary expected at grade level)	The student communicates unclearly.	The student communicates with some clarity and understanding.	The student communicates clearly and precisely.	The student communicates clearly and precisely. The student uses complex forms.
Organization of Ideas	The student organizes incompletely.	The student independently organizes a report.	The student independently organizes a report.	The student organizes a newspaper report.

			The student reports appropriately and logically.	The student reports in complex and logical ways.
Application of Language Conventions (spelling, grammar, punctuation, and style)	The student writes a report with several major errors and/or omissions.	The student writes a report with several minor errors and/or omissions.	The student writes a report with a few minor errors and/or omissions.	The student writes a report with practically no errors and/or omissions.

(2) Norm-referenced Assessment

Norm-referenced assessment (colloquially known as "grading on the curve") is not measured against defined criteria. This type of assessment is relative to the student body undertaking the assessment.

5 Discrete-point vs. Integrative Testing

(1) Discrete-point Testing (e.g., multiple-choice, grammar item)

Language is segmented into many small linguistic points and the four language skills of listening, speaking, reading and writing. Test questions are designed to test these skills and linguistic points. A discrete point test consists of many questions on a large number of linguistic points, but each question tests only one linguistic point. Such tests have a downside in that they take language out of context and usually bear no relationship to the concept or use of the whole language.

(2) Integrative Testing (e.g., interviews, cloze test)

Integrative tests attempt to assess a learner's capacity to use many bits all at the same time, and possibly while exercising several presumed components of a grammatical system, and perhaps more than one of the traditional skills or aspects of skills.

10 \ Types of Assessment according to the Purpose

1] Proficiency Test

The purpose of proficiency test is to test global competence in a language. It tests overall ability regardless of any training they previously had in the language. Proficiency tests have traditionally consisted of the standardized multiple-choices item on grammar, vocabulary, reading comprehension, and listening comprehension. One of the standardized proficiency tests is TOEFL.

2] Diagnostic Test

The purpose is to diagnose specific aspects of a language. These tests offer a checklist of features for the teacher to use in discovering difficulties. This test will typically offer more detailed sub-categorized information on the learner. For example, a writing diagnostic test would first elicit a writing sample of the students. Then, the teacher would identify the organization, content, spelling, grammar, or vocabulary of their writing. Based on that, the teacher can know the needs of students that require a special focus.

3] Placement Test

The purpose of placement test is to place a student into a particular level or section of a language curriculum or school. It usually includes a sampling of the material to be covered in the various courses in a curriculum. A student's performance on the test should indicate the point at which the student will find material neither too easy nor too difficult.

4 Achievement Test

The purpose of achievement tests is to determine whether course objectives have been met with skills acquired by the end of a period of instruction. Achievement tests should be limited to particular material addressed in a curriculum within a particular time frame. Achievement tests belong to summative because they are administered at the end of a unit/term of study. It analyzes the extent to which students have acquired language that has already been taught.

11 \ Intergrative and Alternative Assessment

1 Integrative Test

(1) Cloze Test

In written language, a sentence with a word left out should have enough context that a reader can close that gap with a calculated guess, using linguistic expectancies (formal schemata), background experience (content schemata), and some strategic competence.

① **Types of cloze test**

  ⓐ **Fixed-ratio deletion**: Typically every seventh word (plus or minus two) is deleted.

> **Cloze procedure, fixed-ratio deletion** (every seventh word)
>
> The recognition that one's feelings of (1) _____ and unhappiness can coexist much like (2) _____ and hate in a close relationship (3) _____ offer valuable clues on how to (4) _____ a happier life. It suggests, for (5) _____ that changing or avoiding things that (6) _____ you miserable may well make you (7) _____ miserable but probably no happier.

ⓑ **Rational deletion**: Choose deletions according to the grammatical or discourse functions of the words.

Cloze procedure, rational deletion (prepositions and conjunctions)

The recognition that one's feelings (1) _____ happiness (2) _____ unhappiness can coexist much like love and hate (3) _____ a close relationship may offer valuable clues (4) _____ how to lead a happier life. It suggests, (5) _____ example, that changing (6) _____ avoiding things that make you miserable may well make you less miserable (7) _____ probably no happier.

---

② **Scoring method of cloze tests**

ⓐ **Exact word method**: Students get credit for a correct answer if and only if the word they write in any given blank is the exact word deleted from the original text. This is approach is quick and, therefore, very practical, and also highly reliable.

ⓑ **Acceptable word method**: Any response that is grammatically correct and makes good sense in the context is given full credit as an acceptable answer. This method may promote positive washback, since it could encourage learners to use their pragmatic expectancy grammars creatively.

(2) **C-test**

The second half (according to the number of letters) of every other word is obliterated, and the test-taker must restore each word.

C-test procedure

The recognition th__ one's feel____ of happ_____ and unhap_____ can coe____ much li__ love a__ hate i_ a cl___ relati_____ may of___ valuable cl___ on h __ to le__ a hap____ life. I_ suggests, f__ example, th__ changing o_ avoiding thi___ that ma__ you mise_____ may we__ make y__ less mise_____ but prob_____ no hap_____.

---

2) Alternative Test

(1) Portfolio

Portfolio is a purposeful collection of students' work that demonstrates their efforts, progress, and achievements in given areas. Portfolios include materials such as:

① Essays and compositions in draft and final forms
② Reports, project outlines
③ Poetry and creative prose
④ Artwork, photos, newspaper or magazine clippings
⑤ Audio and/or video recordings of presentations, demonstrations, etc.
⑥ Self and peer-assessments

▶ Potential benefits of portfolios
  • foster intrinsic motivation, responsibility, and ownership,
  • promote student-teacher interaction with the teacher as facilitator,
  • individualize learning and celebrate the uniqueness of each student,
  • provide tangible evidence of a student's work,
  • facilitate critical thinking, self-assessment, and revision processes,
  • opportunities for collaborative work with peers, and
  • permit assessment of multiple dimensions of language learning.

---

(2) Journals

A journal is a log (or "account") of one's thoughts, feelings, reactions, assessments, ideas, or progress toward goals, usually written with little attention to structure, form, or correctness. Learners can articulate their thoughts without the threat of those thoughts being judged later (usually by the teacher).

▶ Dialogue journals: Most classroom-oriented journals are what have now come to be known as dialogue journals. They imply an interaction between a reader (the teacher) and the student through dialogues or responses. For the best results, those responses should be dispersed across a course at regular intervals, perhaps weekly or biweekly. One of the principal objectives in a student's dialogue journal is to carry on a conversation with the teacher.

---

(3) Self-and Peer Assessment

Students are usually frank and honest in their assessment of their own performance and that of their peers. Peer assessment supports students and teachers alike, reduces workload, and increases engagement and understanding. Student insights and observations are valued. They are important because they help the students reflect on and understand the process of their own learning.

12 \ Scoring Method

1) Holistic Scoring Method

Uses a rubric for scoring oral production holistically. Each point on a holistic scale is given a systematic set of descriptors, and the reader-evaluator matches an overall impression with the descriptors to arrive at a score.

Ex

Demonstrates Superiority	5	Strong control of the language; Proficiency and variety in grammatical usage with few significant errors; Broad command of vocabulary and of idiomatic language
Demonstrates Competence	4	Good general control of grammatical structures despite some errors and/or some awkwardness of style; Good use of idioms and vocabulary; Reads smoothly overall.
Suggests Competence	3	Fair ability to express ideas in target language; correct use of simple grammatical structures or use of more complex structures without numerous serious errors; Some apt vocabulary and idioms; Occasional signs of fluency and sense of style
Suggests Incompetence	2	Weak use of language with little control of grammatical structures; Limited vocabulary; Frequent use of anglicisms, which force interpretations on
Demonstrates Incompetence	1	Clearly unacceptable from most points of view; Almost total lack of vocabulary resources, little or no sense of idiom and/or style; Essentially translated from English

2 Analytic Scoring Method

For classroom instruction, holistic scoring provides little washback into the writer's further stages of learning. Classroom evaluation of learning is best served through analytic scoring, in which as many as major elements of writing are scored, thus enabling learners to capture their weaknesses and strengths.

Ex

Grammar	Score
Many Errors	1
Some Errors	2, 3
Few errors	4, 5

Expression	Score
Many anglicisms	1
Acceptable	2, 3
Idiomatic	4, 5

Organization of Ideas	Score
Series of unrelated sentences	1
Coherence between sentences and paragraphs	2, 3
Good coherence between sentences and paragraphs	4, 5

Global Impression	Score
Incomprehensible	1
Acceptable	2, 3
Excellent	4, 5

13 \ Item Analysis

1 Item Facility (Item Difficulty)

Item facility (or IF) is the extent to which an item is easy or difficult for the proposed group of test-takers.

$$Difficulty\ Index = P \text{ or } IF$$
$$0 \leq P \leq 1$$

(0=difficulty item, 1=easy item)
*P = The number of correct responses divided by the number of total test takers

2 Item Discrimination

If a test is given to a large group of people, the discriminating power of an item can be measured by comparing the number of people with high test scores who answered that item correctly with the number of people with low scores who answered the same item correctly. If a particular item is doing a good job of discriminating between those who score high and those who score low, more people in the top-scoring group will have answered the item correctly.

3 Distractor Analysis

Analyzing the distractors (i.e., incorrect alternatives) is useful in determining the relative usefulness of the decoys in each item.

$$D = \% \text{ of upper group} - \% \text{ of lower group}$$

• Positive Item Discrimination Index D •

Group	Item Response			
	A	B	C*	D
Upper group	3	2	15	0
Lower group	12	3	3	2

*denotes correct response

• *Item difficulty*: $(15 + 3)/40 = .45$
• *Discrimination Index*: $(15 - 3)/20 = .60$

• Negative Item Discrimination Index D •

Group	Item Response			
	A	B	C*	D
Upper group	7	5	0	3
Lower group	2	2	10	1

*denotes correct response

• *Item difficulty*: $(0 + 10)/30 = .33$
• *Discrimination Index*: $(0 - 10)/15 = -.67$

Memo

Reference

- 교육부(1997) 제7차 교육과정 중학교 영어과 교육과정 해설, 서울:대한교과서
- 교육부(1997) (제7차) 외국어과 (I), 서울:교육부
- 김영숙 외 5인(1999) 영어과 교육론, 서울:한국문화사
- 김덕기(1998) 영어 교육론, 서울:고려대학교출판부
- 이홍수(1999) 영어 평가 및 멀티미디어 교육론, 서울:한국문화사
- 최연희 외 2인(1998) 열린 교육을 위한 중학교 영어/수학 수행평가의 적용과 효과에 대한 분석 연구, 서울:이화여자대학교사범대학
- Anderson, Anne & Lynch, Tony (2001) Listening:OUP
- Betsy Parrish (2011) Teaching Adult ESL(Practical Introduction):McGrawHill
- Brown, H. Douglas (2000) Principles of Language Learning and Teaching, Fourth Edition:Pearson Education
- Brown, H. Douglas (2001) Teaching by Principles, An Interactive Approach to Language Pedagogy, Second Edition:Pearson Education
- Brown, H. Douglas (2002) Strategies for Success, A Practical Guide to Learning English:Longman
- Brown, H. Douglas (2004) Language Assessment, Principle and Classroom Practices:Longman
- Brumfit, C. J. and Johnson, K (1994) The Communicative Approach to Language Teaching:OUP
- Byrne, Donn (1994) Teaching Oral English, Essex:Longman
- Cross, David (2001) A Practical Handbook Of Language Teaching, Fourth Impression:Longman
- Celce-Murcia, Marianne (2001) Teaching English as a Second or Foreign Language, Third Edition:Heinle & Heinle
- Cook, Guy (2000) Discourse:OUP
- Davies, Paul and Pearse, Eric (2002) Success in English Teaching, Second Impression:OUP
- Ellis, Rod (1999) Understanding Second Language Acquisition:OUP
- Hadley, Alice Omaggio (2001) Teaching Language in Context, Third Edition:Heinle & Heinle
- Heaton, J. B. (1990) Classroom Testing:Longman

- Hedge, Tricia (2000) Teaching and Learning in the Language Classroom:OUP
- Lankshear, Colin, and Michelle Knobel (2006) Digital Literacy and Digital Literacies: Policy, Pedagogy and Research Considerations for Education:Digital Kompetanse
- Larsen-Freeman, Diane (2000) Techniques and Principles in Language Teaching, Second Edition:OUP
- Littlewood, William (1981) Communicative Language Teaching: CUP
- Lightbown and Spada (2003) How Language are Learned, Third Edition:OUP
- Lynch, Tony (1997) Communication in the Language:OUP
- McCarthy, Michael (2001) Discourse Analysis for Language Teachers:CUP
- Nunan, David (2000) Language Teaching Methodology:Pearson Education
- Nunan, David (2003) Practical English Language Teaching:McGraw Hill
- Richard-Amato, Patrica A. (2003) Making It Happen, From Interactive to Participatory Language Teaching, Theory and Practice:Third Edition:Longman
- Richard, Jack C. and Nunan David (1997) Second Language Teacher Education:CUP
- Richard, Jack C. (1995) Understanding Communication In Second Language Classroom:CUP
- Richard, Jack C. and Rogers, Theodore S. (2002) Approaches and Methods in Language Teaching:CUP
- Richard, Jack C. and Schmidt (2002) Dictionary of Language Teaching & Applied Linguistics, Third Edition:Longman
- Shrum, Judith L. and Gilsan, Eileen W. (2000) Teacher's Handbook: Contextualized Language Instruction, Second Edition:Heinle & Heinle
- Teeler, Dede with Gray, Peta (2001) How to Use the Internet in ELT, Third Edition:Longman
- Thornbury, Scott (2000) How to Teach Grammar:Longman
- Thornbury, Scott (2000) How to Teach Vocabulary:Longman
- Ur, Penny (1998) Teaching Listening Comprehension:CUP
- Ur, Penny (2002) A Course in Language Teaching:CUP

NEW

Build Up

박현수 영어교육론 ①-2

Guideline for Pre-service Teachers

Classroom Teaching and Learning

초판인쇄 | 2025. 1. 10.   **초판발행** | 2025. 1. 15.   **편저자** | 박현수

발행인 | 박 용   **발행처** | (주)박문각출판   **표지디자인** | 박문각 디자인팀

등록 | 2015년 4월 29일 제2019-000137호

주소 | 06654 서울시 서초구 효령로 283 서경빌딩   **팩스** | (02)584-2927

전화 | 교재주문·학습문의 (02)6466-7202

저자와의
협의하에
인지생략

정가 31,000원(1, 2권 포함)

ISBN 979-11-7262-418-7 | ISBN 979-11-7262-416-3(세트)